Georgetown University *An Architectural History*

Georgetown University

An Architectural History

STEPHANIE J. RUFINO

With Photographs by Alexis Nollet, AJJN Photography
and Maps by StudioMB

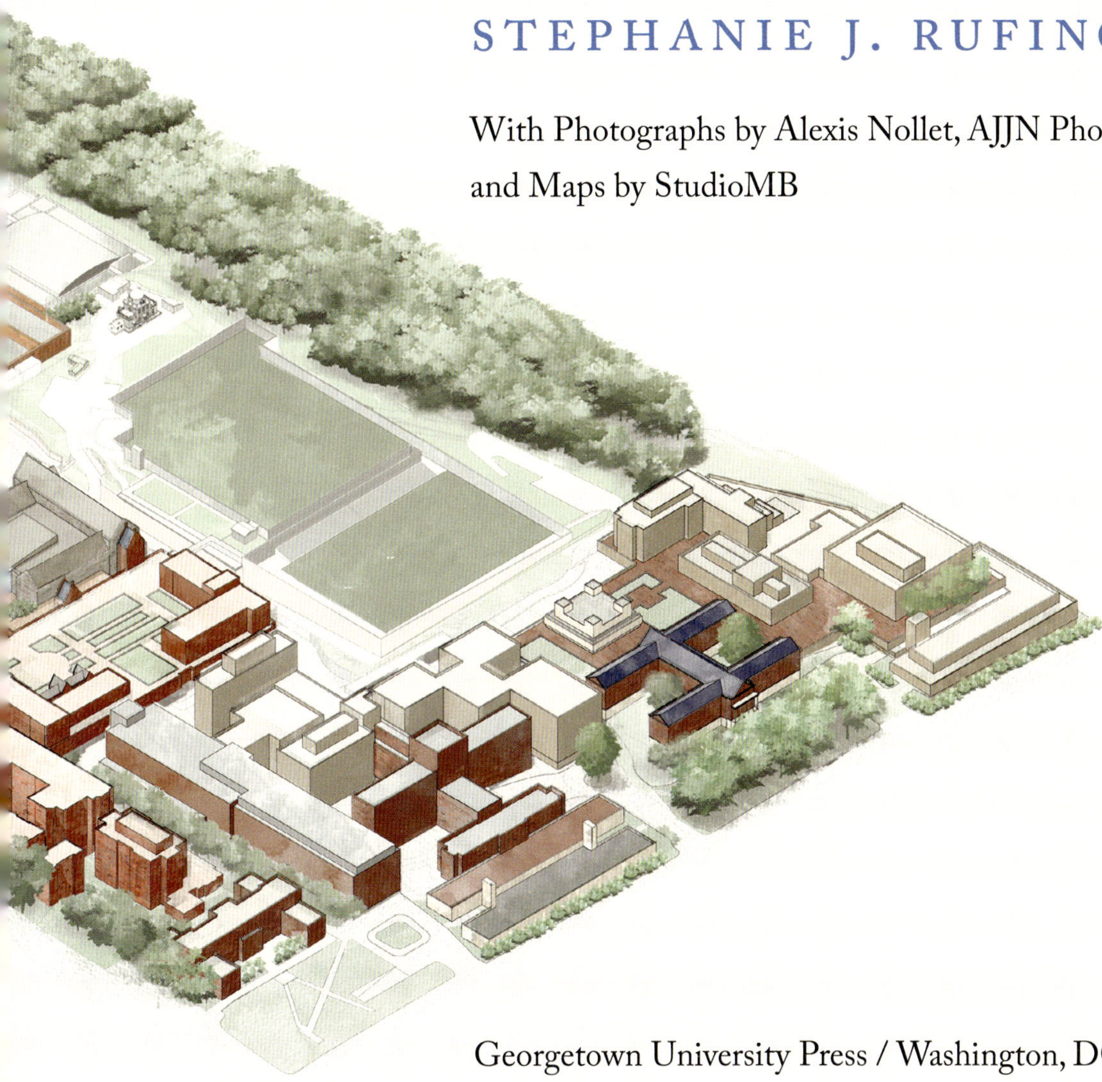

Georgetown University Press / Washington, DC

Except where noted, all contemporary photographs by Alexis Nollet, AJJN Photography.

Library of Congress Cataloging-in-Publication Data

Names: Rufino, Stephanie J., author. | Nollet, Alexis, photographer. | StudioMB (Firm), cartographer.

Title: Georgetown University : an architectural history / Stephanie J. Rufino ; with photographs by Alexis Nollet - AJIN Photography and maps by StudioMB.

Description: Washington, DC : Georgetown University Press, 2025. | Includesbibliographical references.

Identifiers: LCCN 2024021499 (print) | LCCN 2024021500 (ebook) | ISBN 9781647125547 (hardcover) | ISBN 9781647125554 (paperback) | ISBN 9781647125561 (ebook)

Subjects: LCSH: Georgetown University—Buildings—History. | Georgetown University—History. | Architecture—Washington (D.C.)—History. | Washington (D.C.)—Buildings, structures, etc.

Classification: LCC LD1961.G52 R84 2025 (print) | LCC LD1961.G52 (ebook) | DDC 727/.309753—dc23/eng/20250205

LC record available at https://lccn.loc.gov/2024021499

LC ebook record available at https://lccn.loc.gov/2024021500

♾ This paper meets the requirements of ANSI/NISO Z39.48-1992 (Permanence of Paper).

EU GPSR Authorized Representative

LOGOS EUROPE, 9 rue Nicolas Poussin, 17000, LA ROCHELLE, France

Email: *Contact@logoseurope.eu*

26 25 9 8 7 6 5 4 3 2 First printing

Printed in the United States of America

Cover design by Erin Kirk

Interior design by Erin Kirk

This book is dedicated to Jonathan and Amby Rufino

Copley Hall entrance.

Contents

Acknowledgments

Multiple individuals helped in this project's completion. Alexis Nollet, AJJN Photography, completed the building photographs. StudioMB designed the area maps; thank you to Frances Prado and David Bagnoli. Architectural and art historian Dr. Nenette Arroyo contributed building entries of Anne Marie Becraft Hall, Robert and Bernice Wagner Alumni House, the Car Barn, the Law and Medical Centers, the Leo J. O'Donovan Dining Hall, and Wolfington Hall. Dr. Arroyo holds a PhD from the University of Virginia and has recently led courses for Columbia University and the University of Virginia.

A portion of the book's research developed in conjunction with a seminar led for Georgetown's Department of Art and Art History. Students in the course Georgetown University: Architecture & History explored archival materials within the Booth Family Center for Special Collections at Lauinger Library and contributed a select sample of building entries (these contributions are indicated by initials in the text). Thank you in particular to early seminar students Cass Boehm, Andrew Dockser, Gwynne Gershenson, Eliza Lafferty, Matteo Lauto, Carmen Puig Grifoll, Katherine Rangoussis, Grace Ring, Grace Song, and Emma Turner.

I wish to thank Al Bertrand, director of Georgetown University Press, for his consistent project support over the past few years. University archivist Lynn Conway was also immensely helpful in finding a myriad of materials and images for the book and in guiding students through the archives. Thank you also to Ann Galloway, assistant university archivist. The Booth Family Center for Special Collections was a key resource throughout this process, and my students and I enjoyed our time working there. In addition, thank you to the reviewers who provided valuable text suggestions.

A percentage of book sale profits will benefit pediatric oncology departments within Georgetown University Hospital and the University of Chicago Hospital.

Abbreviations

BFCSC	Booth Family Center for Special Collections
C	(Georgetown) College
CAG	Citizens Association of Georgetown
CALL	Capitol Applied Learning Labs
CCC	Concentrated Care Center
GUA	Georgetown University Archives
GUAA	Georgetown University Alumni Association
HFSC	Healey Family Student Center
HUD	US Department of Housing and Urban Development
ICC	Intercultural Center
IHS	Society of Jesus monogram
L	Law School Class of
LEED	Leadership in Energy and Environmental Design
LXR	Loyola/Xavier/Ryder Building
MSB	McDonough School of Business
RAMSA	Robert A. M. Stern Architects
SFS	School of Foreign Service

Introduction

Georgetown University's hilltop site—with Healy Hall's skyline-defining gray towers, the Potomac River to the south, and the entrance lawn's Collegiate Gothic–style buildings neatly arranged to the north—effectively removes the visitor from Washington, DC's downtown persistent buzz. Once a bucolic area northwest of the city, the university's buildings emerged slowly from the late eighteenth century to today and reflect contemporary architectural trends manifest in the nation's capital and beyond. Consisting of roughly 140 acres with strict zoning regulations, the main campus remains constrained by its site boundaries and maximizes all available space. Sustainable design, additional student housing, and expansion beyond the main campus mark recent architectural changes. Amid new strategies and a changing global environment, the university's campus buildings, with their varied style, character, and changing function, continue to form a stalwart backdrop for the development of lifelong friendships and years of learning.

1788–1877: The Early Years

The oldest Catholic university in the United States, Georgetown owes its genesis to John Carroll, SJ (1735–1815). Carroll's vision and drive launched the school and kept the fledgling institution moving ahead in its early years. Born in Maryland, Carroll joined the Jesuit order at age eighteen. He attended universities in France and Belgium, where he studied philosophy and theology. After completing his studies, Carroll remained in Europe, teaching and traveling. In 1774, prompted by Europe's unfavorable climate for Jesuit priests, Carroll returned to Maryland. He served as a leader among priests working to organize the emerging American Catholic Church and was ultimately appointed the first American Catholic bishop in 1790.

During the 1780s Carroll carefully considered the university's site. In a 1786 proposal for the college, Carroll highlighted the "Salubrity of Air,

OPPOSITE: Georgetown College in the District of Columbia. S. Pinistri, Campus in 1829. (Georgetown University Archives)

Aerial view of Georgetown University campus from Virginia.

Georgetown College in the District of Columbia.
S. Pinistri, Campus in 1829. (Georgetown
University Archives)

Convenience of Communication, and Cheapness of Living" as reasons for selecting the Georgetown location. The choice of a removed hilltop site would become common among American colleges in the nineteenth century. Moreover, in comparison to Baltimore or Philadelphia, Georgetown's costs were low. Without the benefit of government sponsorship or a large private endowment, however, financing the school in the early years was a struggle, and Carroll relied on the funds from small donors and revenues earned from the sale of Jesuit-owned lands, where people enslaved by the order toiled in bondage.[1] Carroll distributed his "1786 Proposal for the School" to Catholics in the United States and abroad, in search of individual sponsorship.[2]

Although over ten thousand people live in Georgetown today, during the 1780s the area served as a leading tobacco port and had a population of only roughly two thousand inhabitants. At this time Georgetown's citizenry was approximately one-third Catholic. In 1787, prior to beginning work on the university, Carroll purchased the land for and founded Holy Trinity Church, which continues to thrive just a few blocks east of the university's 37th and O Streets entrance. Beginning in 1788, Carroll oversaw construction of Old South, the university's first building, and in 1789 he received the deed for the school's hilltop land. This first portion of campus land was purchased from Georgetown business and political leaders Col. William Deakins Jr. and John Threlkeld. The historic year of 1789, during which Americans elected George Washington the first president and adopted the US Constitution, marks the university's beginning.

Residing in the western shadow of the iconic Healy Hall (1879), Georgetown's earliest brick structures now appear dwarfed by centuries of growth. At the time, however, beyond Georgetown and across the capital few other large-scale buildings competed with the university's colossal Old North (1795). Old North stretches over 150 feet east to west. The US Capitol Building, the White House, and the no-longer-extant Blodgett's Hotel were among the small number of Washington, DC, structures that rivaled Old North in size. Using a grand scale for an educational building was not unique to Georgetown, however, as Old North is similar to Princeton University's Nassau Hall (1756), one of the largest buildings in the English colonies in the mid-eighteenth century.[3] Though Nassau Hall is closer in design to Old North, Harvard University's Massachusetts Hall (1720) and Yale University's Connecticut Hall (1750–52) provide additional early college hall precedents.

Georgetown's early buildings served many purposes. Though no longer standing, and with Ryan Hall (built in 1905) now residing on its site, students studied, ate, and lived in the small gable-roofed Old South. Old North also served multiple functions: It included classrooms, a chapel, a museum, a library, the president's office, and dormitory space. For over thirty

South View of Georgetown College 1875 (From actual measurement). J. L. Smithmeyer & Co. Architects. (Georgetown University Art Collection)

J. L. Smithmeyer & Co.
Archite
etown College 1875.
easurement.)

years campus activities centered between the Old North and Old South Buildings, with the campus oriented toward the Potomac River.

In 1791 William Gaston, Georgetown College's first enrolled student, arrived at the college, and by 1810 some forty-three students were enrolled at the nascent school.[4] When Gaston arrived at Georgetown he was only thirteen years old. Gaston's young age highlights that during the school's early years there were three divisions—elementary, preparatory, and collegiate, with the elementary level open to students as young as eight years old.

Following construction of the Old South and Old North Buildings in the early nineteenth century, to the west of Old South the college added to the hilltop site the Infirmary (now Gervase Hall) (1830) and Isaac Hawkins Hall (built in 1832 under a different name). Designed expressly for the younger students, Maguire Hall opened to the east of Old South in 1854.

Though long forgotten, the campus "Walks" were integral to the university's nineteenth-century landscape. Joseph West, a Maryland farmer and Jesuit priest, laid the serpentine plan for the Walks, also referred to as the Mile Path, in the 1820s. It began near today's White-Gravenor Hall (1933), stretched northward, and then looped back toward Old North. Oak, poplar,

Midway of the Walks, with college buildings to the left. 1874. (Georgetown University Archives)

Cars parked outside Healy Hall. Photograph by John Brosnan, SJ, 1915. (Georgetown University Archives)

and beech trees lined the paths, where students often escaped to enjoy time with friends. Bridges spanning small creeks, its peaceful solitude, and lush forest areas away from campus professors and adult supervision mark the nineteenth-century descriptions of the paths.[5] In 1873 a writer for the *College Journal* warned, regarding the Walks, "May the hand of man ever respect this unique creation."[6] Nonetheless, the expanding institution, coupled with the early twentieth-century rise of the automobile, meant that interest in and use of the Walks waned. The construction of Copley Hall (1932) began the gradual elimination of the labyrinthine wooded campus escape.

To the west of the Walks and beyond the school's core structures, the Heyden Observatory provided a pivotal mid-nineteenth-century addition to campus. Although now appearing as a diminutive domed relic on the edge of a fully twenty-first-century campus, the 1844 Observatory housed scientific facilities that produced pioneering work and remained a vibrant campus structure for much of the twentieth century. Completed during the presidency of James Ryder, SJ (1840–45 and 1848–51), the Heyden was one of the earliest college observatories in the country. James Curley, SJ (1796–1889) founded and designed the Observatory. Originally from Ireland, Curley in 1831 began a long career teaching science at Georgetown. Working together with scientists in England and Washington, DC, Curley calculated the earliest longitude and latitude measurements of the Observatory and other important sites in the nation's capital. The building now commemorates Francis J. Heyden, SJ, who led the Observatory from 1948 to 1972.

Jesuit Community Cemetery.

Also key to the university's earliest years and unique for an American college, the Jesuit Community Cemetery lies east of Heyden Observatory, near the center of campus. Begun in 1808, the university moved the cemetery to its current location in 1854. Construction of Maguire Hall, close to the cemetery's original position west of Healy Hall, prompted the move. Resting in a low, once-isolated area, campus development now surrounds the cemetery. Buried here are over 350 members of the Jesuit community, including some seventeen former Georgetown presidents. In 1964 Georgetown's business vice president, T. Byron Collins, SJ, investigated the cost of moving the interred to a Maryland site in order to free up this prime central campus land, but the initiative did not move forward given the legal and moral issues involved.[7]

The university's early history is intertwined with the era of slavery, and the institution continues to reconcile with its past. Until recently the building sitting perpendicular to the school's early infirmary commemorated former Georgetown president Thomas Mulledy (1829–38 and 1845–48), who as provincial superior of the Maryland Jesuits led the notorious 1838 sale of 272 enslaved individuals, many of whom were transported to work on plantations in Louisiana. The residence has been renamed and rededicated to Isaac Hawkins, a sixty-five-year-old enslaved man whose name was listed first on the 1838 bill of sale of the enslaved. Before the rededication to Hawkins in 2015, student protests led to the removal of Mulledy's name and the building was initially renamed Freedom Hall.

To orchestrate the egregious 1838 sale, which broke apart many enslaved families, Mulledy worked together with William McSherry, SJ, Georgetown president from 1838 to 1839. The enslaved individuals were sold to plantation owners Henry Johnson and Jesse Batey in Louisiana. The price of the enslaved individuals was set at over $100,000 (more than $3 million today, adjusted for inflation). Despite rising student enrollment during Mulledy's presidency, the college faced severe financial challenges during the 1830s, which were in part due to the building of Gervase and Isaac Hawkins Halls. Initial efforts by Mulledy to secure loans to pay for the building failed, and by 1838 the college had accumulated significant debt. The sale of the 272 Maryland slaves became in Mulledy's mind increasingly important to the college's financial survival.

In the spring of 2017, during a courtyard ceremony in the company of more than one hundred descendants of these enslaved individuals, Georgetown University formally apologized for its role in the 1838 sale, and the former Mulledy Building was rededicated as Isaac Hawkins Hall. Earlier student protests in 2015 led to the renaming of nearby McSherry Hall (1792) to Remembrance Hall, which in 2017 was also rededicated to Anne Marie Becraft (1805–33), a pioneering African American educator. Becraft founded one of the first schools for Black girls in Georgetown and became one of the first Black nuns in America. The memorializing of Isaac Hawkins and Anne Marie Becraft plays an important part in the university's ongoing effort to reconcile with the institution of slavery and its role in the 1838 sale.

Enslaved individuals played a role in the early life and development of the campus. They worked on campus, and a significant portion of the student population came from slaveholding families. During Georgetown's first three decades, the school hired and exploited the labor of up to twelve enslaved people per year, to work in activities like construction, maintenance, and operations. Jesuits rented enslaved individuals from parents of students and alumni, completing tasks such as laying bricks and hauling materials, the college employed enslaved laborers to build Old North and expand the campus in the early nineteenth century.[8] The college's early leaders were connected to slavery in multiple ways. John Carroll owned at least one slave, while Ryder spoke against abolition.[9] Other physical reminders of the university's past remain. Above White-Gravenor Hall's western entrance is a crest memorializing Br. Joseph Mobberly, SJ, an overseer at Maryland's Saint Inigoes manor plantation and later a Georgetown instructor. In the 1820s, amid abolitionist arguments against slavery, Mobberly continued using racist ideology to justify the institution, claiming that people of African descent were inferior. He was eventually dismissed from Saint Inigoes following complaints over his brutal treatment of others.[10]

Georgetown was embedded in the regime of slavery, and the Civil War impacted the campus's later nineteenth-century development. More than a thousand Georgetown alumni served in the war, with the majority fighting for the Confederacy. An 1861 illustration in *Harper's Weekly* magazine depicts

Union soldiers gathered in front of Old South, as the US government used campus buildings for housing and hospitalization during the war.[11]

Georgetown's Medical and Law Schools emerged before and after the Civil War, respectively. The Medical School began in 1849 and classes launched soon thereafter. First located at the corner of F and 12th Streets downtown, the Medical Department later resided at a 10th and E Street site and also occupied a building on H Street, before moving to the main campus in 1930. Founded in 1870, after a series of early downtown building shifts, the Law School moved into its longtime home at 506 E Street NW in 1891. The Law School remained at its E Street location until 1971, when it moved to its current 600 New Jersey Avenue building, designed by celebrated American architect Edward Durell Stone (1902–78).

Old South Building. Illustrated in "Our Army at Washington," *Harpers Weekly*, June 1, 1861.

Georgetown College with Healy Hall, Old North, and Ryan Gymnasium. Postcard ca. 1920. (Georgetown University Archives)

1878–1935: Building Under Presidents Healy, Richards, and Nevils

The development of Healy Hall, Dahlgren Chapel, and the later adjacent quadrangle to the north marked campus construction during the late nineteenth and early twentieth centuries. Referred to as the university's second founder, Patrick Healy (president 1874–82) transformed the university. In addition to raising funds for Healy Hall and overseeing its development, Healy implemented more strenuous graduation requirements, bolstered the professional schools, and placed greater emphasis on the study of science. Enrollment increased under Healy. By 1882 over two hundred students were enrolled in the college, plus twenty-six medical and forty-five law students. Described as a temperamental yet polished diplomat, Healy came to Georgetown in 1866 as chair of the Philosophy Department and later rose to dean of the college.[12] The son of an enslaved woman and an Irish-born cotton planter from Georgia, Healy is now sometimes celebrated as the first African American president of an American university. At the time, however, Healy concealed his Black ancestry.[13]

Healy Hall remains Healy's leading contribution to the university's development. Now a globally recognized building, Healy Hall's expansive eastern facade boldly marks the university's entrance within the 37th and O Street gates. By siting Healy Hall to face east, the orientation of the campus shifted dramatically toward the capital, as the university grew in strength and importance. The hall's form rejects the earlier Federal architectural style of the surrounding brick structures and reflects the more diverse, cosmopolitan aesthetic present in late nineteenth-century American architecture.

Noted US Library of Congress architects John L. Smithmeyer (1832–1908) and Paul Pelz (1841–1918) designed Healy Hall. Immigrants to this country, Smithmeyer hailed from Vienna and Pelz from Prussia; both were skilled at working in European architectural styles. Healy Hall is predominantly Romanesque Revival in style. Its large scale, rounded arches, rusticated stone, and bifora windows are all characteristic of the Romanesque Revival mode. An early variant of this form is the Rundbogenstil ("round arch") style, which has German roots and was popular in American design beginning in the mid-nineteenth century. Richard Upjohn's Bowdoin College chapel (1855) exemplifies the use of the Rundbogenstil style in American collegiate architecture. Aspects of Upjohn's chapel, such as the rusticated stone and window design, are evident in Healy Hall. Emblematic of Healy's eclectic nature, its stepped roof gable and Gothic ornamentation also echo G. G. Scott's Victorian-era St. Pancras Station in London (1868–74).

After its initial opening in 1879, Healy Hall continued to evolve to meet the school's growing needs. During the presidency of J. Havens Richards, SJ (1888–98), Riggs Memorial Library opened within Healy Hall in 1891; and

Collage of university buildings pictured in the *Georgetown College Yearbook* 1916. (Georgetown University Archives)

Br. Francis Schroen, SJ, oversaw completion of the interior decoration of Gaston Hall Auditorium in 1901.

President Richards was also instrumental in the development of Dahlgren Chapel (1893) and the building of the university's early hospital along N Street on the east campus. Richards convinced Elizabeth and John Dahlgren (C 1889, L 1891) to fund the compact Gothic Revival–style chapel, which rests at the core of the quadrangle behind Healy Hall. Dahlgren Chapel, designed by architect Henry Simpson, echoes earlier chapels of a similar style, such as James Renwick Jr.'s Oak Hill Cemetery Chapel (1850) in Georgetown. Upjohn employed a similar tri-lobed ceiling interior in his earlier church work in Raleigh, North Carolina. Dahlgren Chapel's richly hued stained glass window depictions of various Catholic pioneers exemplify the religious imprint evident in the ornament of multiple campus buildings.

Given the broad campus architectural trends taking hold at the time, the U-shaped configuration of Georgetown's early buildings resonates. Hawkins Hall, Old South, and Maguire Hall form the historic core's south side, with Healy Hall to the east joining Old North. The work of architect Benjamin Henry Latrobe (1764–1820) provides one precedent for such a configuration. Latrobe, an Englishman who came to America in 1795, had significant influence on early American campus design. Along with work on the US Capitol, the White House, Lafayette Square buildings, and other designs, Latrobe contributed to the form of at least eight American colleges, including the University of Virginia. In 1816 Latrobe drew a U-shaped plan for a proposed national university to be located on the Washington Mall. This unrealized

OPPOSITE: *The New South Hall Georgetown College Journal*, March 1905. (Georgetown University Archives)

plan boasted a central building (which included a library and refectory) flanked by lodging and lecture spaces.[14] Latrobe's placement of a church opposite the proposed university's central building foreshadows the placement of Dahlgren Chapel on axis with Healy Hall. As Paul Turner has observed, Latrobe's use of connected buildings in his college designs contrasted with other early American campus plans composed of separate buildings, as seen in the late eighteenth and early nineteenth-century plans for the University of North Carolina and Harvard University.[15] John Trumbull's (1756–1843) late eighteenth-century plans for Yale's Old Brick Row, likely the oldest surviving master plan for an American college, provides a model of linearly arranged buildings. Yale's structures, however, stood separate from one another.[16] Latrobe's concept for a national university having connected elements provides one precedent for the cohesive, albeit slowly evolving arrangement of Georgetown University's historic core.

In the early twentieth century multiple new buildings emerged within the historic core area. Ryan Hall made headlines in 1905, with the *Washington Post* characterizing it as "one of the most up-to-date college buildings of its kind." Designed by A. O. Von Herbulis (1861–1928) and built on the former site of Old South, Ryan Hall possesses a layered profile with a base arcade,

Athletic Field Georgetown University, Washington, D.C. The field later became Copley Lawn. Postcard ca. 1915. (Georgetown University Archives)

classical columns, pilasters, and dormer windows. This rather exuberant small building echoes various late nineteenth-century architectural trends. Its contrasting white colonnade and red brick arcade echo features of Ernest Flagg's Bourne Residence in New York (1897). Flagg's building references the Neo-Palladian tradition of Georgian England. Ryan Hall's layered effect also echoes, in small measure, the Second Empire architectural style seen in structures such as the sprawling, flamboyant Eisenhower Executive Office Building in Washington, DC (1888).

After the construction of Ryan Hall, the historic campus core expanded again in the post–World War I era. Georgetown enrollments surged following the war, and there were close to nine hundred students enrolled in the college by the mid-1920s. To house additional students, in 1926 New North opened adjacent to Old North, effectively extending the earlier structure.

Despite the pressures of leading the school during the Great Depression, President W. Coleman Nevils, SJ (1928–35) managed to complete a herculean campus building campaign during his tenure. Moreover, Nevils expanded Georgetown's reputation and connections, giving the university newfound visibility in the nation's capital. Nevils reached out to the political, ecclesiastic, and intellectual communities of Washington, DC, in an unprecedented manner and led in the development of the "Greater Georgetown" plan.[17]

Nevils's transformative plan included replacement of an early athletic field with the Andrew White Memorial Quadrangle, anchored by Copley Hall to the west and White-Gravenor Hall to the north. Though unrealized due to Depression-era financial constraints, Nevils's plan also included the design of an additional building on the quadrangle's eastern side. Andrew White, along with John Gravenor and Thomas Copley, were Jesuits who left England and came to Maryland in the 1630s. Nevils's strategic naming of multiple buildings after early Jesuit leaders implicitly pushed the origins of the university back in time, thereby bolstering its perceived historic roots.

Working with architect Emile Perrot (1872–1954), Nevils very closely managed the development of the quadrangle buildings. Born in Philadelphia, Perrot attended the University of Pennsylvania and in 1920 started his own design practice. Although adept at the medieval-inspired Collegiate Gothic style, Perrot embraced new building technologies and was a pioneer in the use of concrete reinforced with steel.

Despite its open eastern side, Perrot's quadrangle plan in part echoes the City Beautiful urban planning movement that took hold across the country in the early twentieth century. The World's Columbian Exposition, held in Chicago in 1893, marked the beginning of the City Beautiful movement in America. Reiterating the balance and order of the Chicago fair's buildings and grounds, architects of the time reenvisioned the design of large

Reproduction of "Aerial View of Greater Georgetown." Emile Perrot, 1929. (Georgetown University Archives)

Aerial
View of
Greater
George
Town

cities—such as Washington, DC, and Chicago—with clear axes and ordered green spaces. On a micro scale, the penchant for order and clarity, as well as for similarly styled grouped buildings, manifested on the American campus. A clear parallel for such Beaux Arts planning is evident in the early twentieth-century work of architects Émile Bénard and Galen Howard at the University of California, Berkeley. At Georgetown, the front quadrangle's lawn and Perrot's cohesive Collegiate Gothic style buildings echo the clarity and order inherent in the City Beautiful movement.

It was also under Nevils that the Medical School's flagship structure emerged on Reservoir Road in 1930. Although the University Hospital (1898) existed on the eastern side of campus, Nevils realized the Medical School's future development would need significant space, which the then-undeveloped northwest campus area would provide.

Georgetown's later development occurred in parallel with the growth of other Jesuit institutions. In particular, the campus layout contrasts with the layout of Boston College but shares affinity with the layout of New York City's Fordham University. Boston College, founded by Jesuits in 1863 (more than seventy years after Georgetown's founding), possesses the first comprehensive master plan for a Catholic college campus. The leading architectural firm of Maginnis & Walsh, designers of Washington's colossal Basilica of the National Shrine of the Immaculate Conception (ca. 1919–59), created the Boston College plan, employing the Collegiate Gothic style. Between 1909 and 1959 the Maginnis firm built eleven buildings for Boston College, far more than any single architect had contributed to Georgetown's campus. A notable connection exists, however, between Georgetown and Fordham in the work of architect Emile Perrot. Prior to designing Copley and White-Gravenor Halls, Perrot contributed to a significant Fordham building campaign, designing a library and a science building and renovating a church for the New York campus.[18]

World War II, Development Under President Bunn, and Beyond

World War II significantly affected the university, and the campus continued to transform. Amid the war, the university received government funds for new buildings and later repurposed war structures for educational use. Government money supported the opening of a new hospital on Reservoir Road in 1948. Following the war, university enrollments skyrocketed across the country as the GI Bill paid tuition and other expenses for millions of returning veterans. By 1946–47 the college's enrollment was close to fifteen hundred, and the School of Foreign Service had a thousand students, many of whom were veterans. Poulton Hall, located beyond Copley lawn on 37th

Street, is a World War II surplus structure. During the war this building served as part of a Pennsylvania TNT manufacturing plant, and the university later moved it to campus.

During the post–World War II era, the leadership of President Edward Bunn, SJ, had a phenomenal impact on the campus's development. Characterized as a particularly accessible leader, Bunn led the university from 1952 to 1964. During his tenure, enrollment increased dramatically, from just over forty-nine hundred students in 1952 to close to seventy-five hundred students by 1964. Like Nevils before him, Bunn's building campaign enormously changed the campus. Among the structures completed during Bunn's term are the McDonough Gymnasium (1952), the Edmund A. Walsh Memorial Building for the School of Foreign Service (1958), the New South dormitory and cafeteria (1958), and the Reiss Science Building (1962), the latter of which was built over a cemetery that included the graves of multiple enslaved individuals. Among the interred was Margaret Smallwood, who labored in slavery at the college before dying in 1837.[19]

The medical and nursing buildings that emerged at this time were Saint Mary's Hall (1956), the Gorman Building (1959), and the no-longer-extant Kober-Cogan Building (1959). During Bunn's presidency and following the launch of the first *Sputnik* space capsule by the Soviet Union in 1957, the US government increasingly channeled funds to universities and their building programs in an effort to bolster American education. Government funding played a role in the development and construction of multiple buildings on campus during the later twentieth century, including the New South, Reiss, and Gorman Buildings.

Bunn led the school during the early 1960s, an era of change across American campuses. Georgetown finally became a fully coeducational institution in 1969, when the university admitted women to the College of Arts and Sciences. Georgetown's first high-rise structures, Darnall Hall and Harbin Hall, originally for female and male students, respectively, emerged in the mid-1960s. Using minimal ground space, both buildings helped meet the university's seemingly perennial pressing need for more on-campus housing. Given Harbin's site within the inner campus and Darnall's far to the north, near Reservoir Road, the structures' placement underscores the fledgling position of women on campus at the time.

1970 to Today: Libraries, Housing, and Sustainable Design

Over the last fifty-plus years, university leaders added a myriad of new structures to the hilltop. Among the notable developments during this later era are the Joseph Mark Lauinger Memorial Library (1970) and many residence halls: Henle Village (1976, majority demolished in 2023), Village A (1979),

Harbin Hall. Photograph by Campbell Photo Service, ca. 1965.
(Georgetown University Archives)

Alumni Square (1983), Village C (1987), and Southwest Quadrangle (2003). A student center, as well as new buildings for the School of Foreign Service, for the McDonough School of Business, and for the sciences all emerged in this later era and filled in the campus's central and western landscape. Residence halls added in 2003, along with a new athletic center, saturated the once-open southwest area of campus.

A leading national architect working on campus in the 1970s, John Carl Warnecke (1919–2010) was a pioneer in the burgeoning historic preservation movement and celebrated for his contextual approach to design. Warnecke worked with First Lady Jacqueline Kennedy to preserve structures within Lafayette Square. Along with designing several notable Washington, DC, government buildings, Warnecke designed President John F. Kennedy's memorial gravesite at Arlington National Cemetery.

On campus, Warnecke & Associates designed Lauinger Library and residence halls Henle Village and Village A on the north and south side

Lauinger Library model. Photograph by Louis Checkman, ca. 1966. (Georgetown University Archives)

of campus, respectively. Lauinger exemplifies the then–en vogue Brutalist mode. This style has multiple roots, but a key precedent resides in the post–World War II concrete architecture of Swiss architect Charles-Édouard Jeanneret, known as Le Corbusier (1887–1965). Brutalism's name derives from the French "béton brut," or "rough concrete." In general, large-scale geometric concrete forms and open, expansive interior spaces characterize Brutalist buildings. Sensitively varied concrete textures also mark the style. These structures, popular during the 1960s and 1970s, appear awkwardly grand and unaffected, in stark contrast to the sleek, aloof International style glass-and-steel skyscrapers of the 1950s.

Prior to Warnecke's Lauinger Library, the Brutalist mode made a splash in the nation's capital, most notably with Marcel Breuer and Herbert Beckhard's Housing and Urban Development Building (1963–68), while C. F. Murphy's J. Edgar Hoover / FBI Building (1967–72) was also underway. The Lauinger Library also echoes similarly styled structures appearing on other American campuses at the time, such as architect Walter Netsch's Brutalist libraries at the University of Chicago and Northwestern University (both built in 1970). Lauinger's side-flanged walls recall Luigi Moretti's influential Casa Girasole (1950) in Rome. Moretti designed Washington, DC's Watergate Complex (1971), while Moretti's Casa Girasole, a forerunner of the Postmodern movement in architecture, received considerable discussion by Robert Venturi in his influential text *Complexity and Contradiction in Architecture* (1966).

Certainly, Lauinger Library reflects its era, and its design emerged within a broader evolution of library architecture on American campuses. Historian Dale Allen Gyure observes a "golden age" of university library construction that took hold from the late nineteenth century to World War II, exemplified by structures such as Columbia University's Neoclassical Low Memorial Library designed by McKim, Mead & White (1895). During this time, the grand, monumental Low Library assumed a central position on campus, as had the earlier Riggs Memorial Library within the envelope of Healy Hall. By the 1950s, however, a general shift away from unified campus plans and hierarchical structures occurred. Efficiency increasingly outweighed revival aesthetics. Simplified, more flexible, and more modular, these new library plans emerged that, as with Lauinger, integrated book stacks and reading areas. This architectural shift occurred amid a broad democratization of higher education, with widespread enrollment increases and students coming from far more diverse economic and cultural backgrounds in pursuit of university degrees.[20]

Along with the main campus's Lauinger Library, on the north medical campus is the Brutalist style Dahlgren Memorial Library (1971), which, as Cass Boehm (C 2020) has observed, resides on its site like a "pillbox bunker

Dahlgren Memorial Library on the Medical Center campus. Photograph by J. Russell Lawrence, ca. 1970. (Georgetown University Archives)

of France's Maginot Line." Both the main and medical campus libraries stand next to revival-style buildings, which contrast with their later heavy concrete forms and further prompt critical barbs from students preferring the historical mode.

Despite delving into a host of divergent architectural styles and trends over the years, various elaborate campus designs have remained at least partially unrealized. During the 1980s, university architect Dean Price developed plans for terraced buildings enclosing a central rectangular courtyard and descending south toward the Potomac River. Price's plan included a tall bell tower, a domed theater, and connecting arcades running east to west. In small measure, Thomas Jefferson's sloped lawn at the University of Virginia inspired Price's urban model. Despite its extravagance, aspects of Price's plan certainly took hold, including the central green courtyard that extends from Leavey Student Center (1988) and is flanked by the Rafik B. Hariri Building (2009), which houses the McDonough School of Business, and Regents Hall (2012) housing science. The 2005 development of the Davis Performing Arts Center by noted architect Hugh Hardy (1932–2017) also references Price's plan, though in a much more conservative manner.

Preliminary design by university architect Dean Price for the proposed Intermodal Transportation Center, 1985. (Courtesy Planning and Facilities Management)

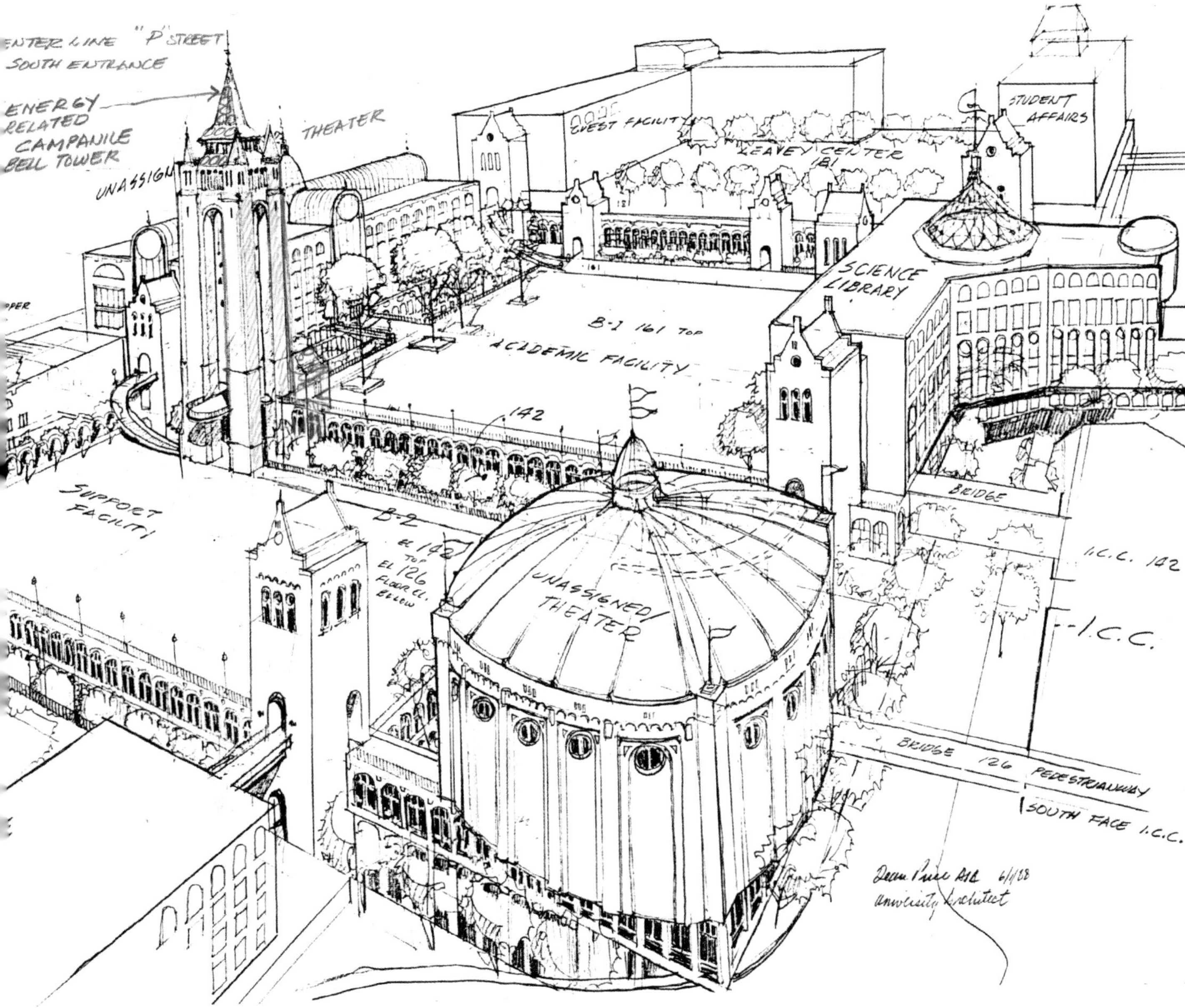

Preliminary design by university architect Dean Price for a series of proposed buildings to the south of Leavey Student Center, 1988. (Courtesy Planning and Facilities Management)

In the 1980s Price also proposed a central, historically inspired transportation hub close to the university's southern Canal Road entrance. The architect envisioned that the university's bus system, the city's Metrobus line, and an electric trolley-like system would all pass through the spot. Price was future-focused and a keen proponent of the use of solar energy on campus. Even so, the architectural design of his planned transportation hub harkens back to Classical and Renaissance designs with scalloped shell sculpture niches and coffered ceilings supported by no less than fluted Corinthian columns.

During the presidency of Timothy S. Healy, SJ (1976–89), the university's endowment soared and building construction marched on. Hugh Newell Jacobsen (1929–2021), a local architect with a celebrated national reputation, designed the brick residence halls of Alumni Square (1983), which mimic the surrounding Georgetown historic row houses. In the later twentieth century Postmodern architects jettisoned the rigidity of the streamlined glass-and-steel International style prevalent in the postwar years. In defiance of the International mode, Postmodernists often looked back to historical forms and ornament in an exaggerated manner. At the Alumni Square site, Jacobsen subtly integrated this approach, given the residence hall's historically inspired yet slightly overscaled corbelled cornice and oriel windows. At the building's corner, in a tongue-in-cheek nod characteristic of many Postmodern designs, Jacobsen incorporated a broken cornice and oddly placed gutter.

Along with an increasing need for student housing in the 1980s, the university added two key structures within its core space below the northern medical complex: the Edward B. Bunn, SJ Intercultural Center (ICC) (1982) and the Leavey Student Center (1988). The ICC, which houses the School of Foreign Service, demonstrates the university's pioneering approach to sustainable architecture in its colossal solar roof. Just north of the ICC, the Leavey Student Center emerged as a multipurpose complex, including a hotel, a faculty club, a bookstore, several eateries, and more. Designed by Mariani & Associates, the center aimed to reduce "town-gown" tensions via its parking and hotel accommodations within the campus center.

The university's continual drive to increase campus housing spaces, beginning in the later twentieth century and continuing today, underscores the fact that a core principle of the American university's mission is to provide the opportunity for students to live closely together. As Benjamin Franklin, a University of Pennsylvania founder, noted, students should attend college to "zealously unite."[21] Today the university has numerous projects to increase student housing spaces on the main campus. This has led to the recent demolition of the majority of Henle Village, which is being replaced with a larger residence hall, while the Leavey Center's hotel now functions as student housing.

Moreover, in recent years the university has strengthened its connection to the city by developing its Capitol Campus. Located near the US Capitol

Exterior of Healey Family Student Center. Photograph by Brad Feinknopf, 2014.

Building, this satellite campus extends outward from Georgetown's Law Center. Among the Capitol Campus buildings is a residence hall at 55 H Street, designed by Robert A. M. Stern Architects (RAMSA). Along with modern apartments, this eleven-story structure includes amenity and academic spaces on the lower floors and two outside courtyards. Also RAMSA-designed, the Capitol Campus's 125 E Street building houses the McCourt School of Public Policy and serves as a downtown anchor. Celebrated designer Maya Lin (b. 1959) created multiple works of art for this uplifting, light-filled modern structure close to the US Capitol. With over 130,000 square feet of classroom, office, and lounge spaces, 125 E Street also incorporates an auditorium and rooftop event and terrace space. On the same block as the Law Center and not far from the H Street building, 125 E Street connects to the 500 First Street building. Students in the university's Capitol Applied Learning Labs (CALL) Program use both the 55 H Street and 500 First Street structures, as they spend a semester living, studying, and working downtown. Also nearby and contributing to the Capitol Campus is the 111 Massachusetts Avenue building, which the university acquired in 2021 and houses interdisciplinary programs. Beyond its growing, cohesive presence near the Capitol, the university also maintains an exceedingly strong global presence through its study and experience abroad programs in many foreign countries.

The university remains focused on developing environmentally sound buildings. Campus structures receiving platinum, gold, or silver LEED ratings (Leadership in Energy and Environmental Design, awarded by the US Green Building Council) have sprouted across campus; award-winning designs include Regents Hall; the Rafik B. Hariri Building; Pedro Arrupe, SJ Residence Hall; Nevils Hall; Leo J. O'Donovan Dining Hall; and the John R. Thompson Jr. Intercollegiate Athletic Center. In addition, the Capitol Campus's 55 H Street building received a platinum LEED certification. Among the university's common sustainability strategies is the adaptive reuse of existing structures to new purpose, as exemplified by the Healey Family Student Center within New South and the conversion of the historic Ryan and Isaac Hawkins Halls into undergraduate residences. Incorporation of "green" walls and roofs, solar panels, the capture and reuse of rainwater, and permeable walkway pavers, which filter and redirect stormwater, are all elements of the university's sustainable building strategies.

Despite the many shifts and turns in development under a host of presidents over time, there is a cohesion in the hilltop's built collage. Forms and materials throughout the campus echo one another and create visual connections across time, as architects have deliberately gestured to older forms while looking toward the future. The frequently employed red brick functions as a visual connector. Village A's vertical, abstract geometric projections echo that of the adjacent Lauinger Library. The Leavey Student Center's late twentieth-century towers, with their stepped gables and round arches, allude to Healy Hall's western facade. Arrupe Hall's lightly colored stone continues the hues of the Depression-era White-Gravenor Hall, while Stern's colossal southwest quadrangle dorms with their sharp gables gesture to the roofline of Copley Hall and other early structures.

Woven together, multiple buildings reach out visually to the city. Arrupe Hall's seventh floor vista frames a sweeping view of the Capitol and the Washington Monument. Warnecke sensitively captured the Kennedy Center and Potomac River view from Lauinger's fifth floor Murray Room, while fragments of a capital city map, harkening back to Pierre Charles L'Enfant's 1791 city plan, decorate the Hariri Building's exterior. Students come and live in this tightly integrated main campus and forge lasting friendships. Gaining insight into the campus's architectural evolution enables the student, alumnus, or visitor to more deeply sense the physical spaces here and appreciate the environment that enables those bonds and learning.

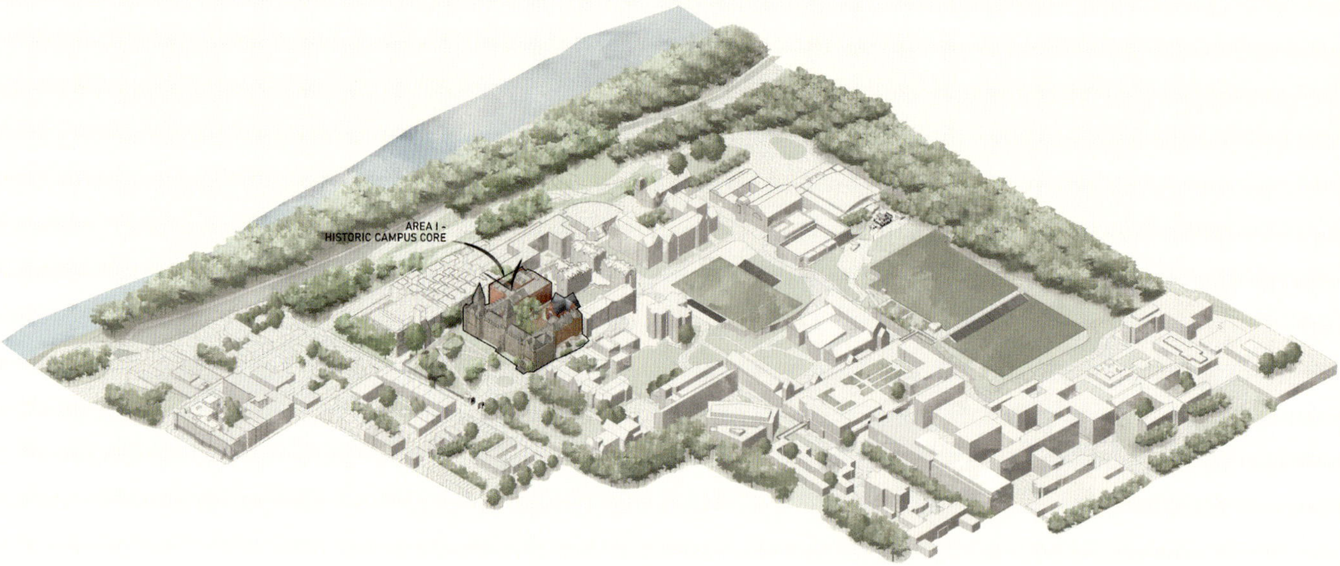
AREA I -
HISTORIC CAMPUS CORE

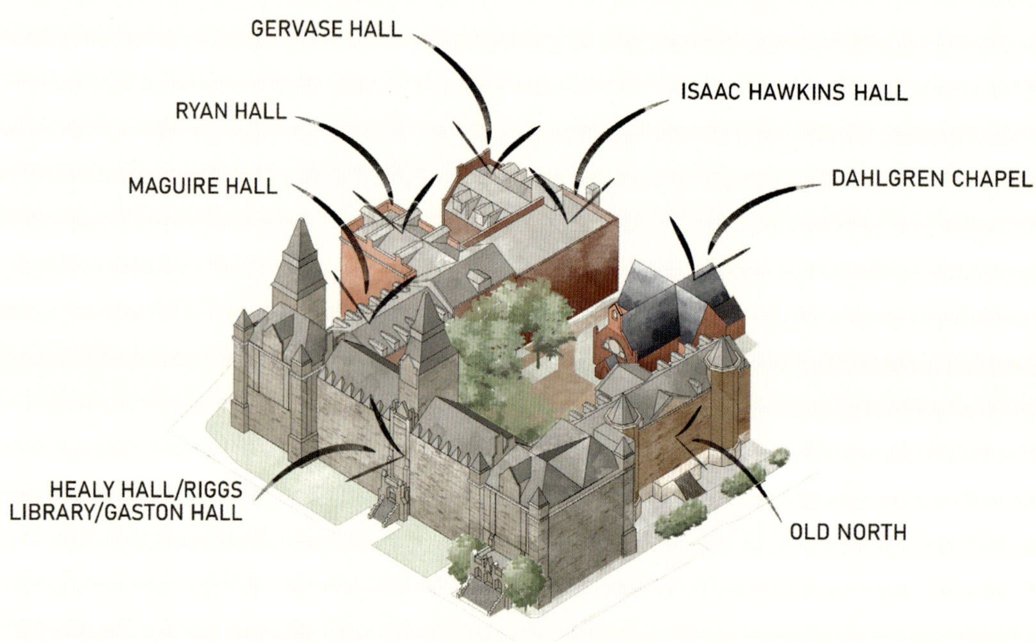
GERVASE HALL
ISAAC HAWKINS HALL
RYAN HALL
MAGUIRE HALL
DAHLGREN CHAPEL
HEALY HALL/RIGGS
LIBRARY/GASTON HALL
OLD NORTH

Historic Campus Core

The university's core historic structures stand behind Healy Hall (1879) and date back to the late eighteenth century. Built with red brick and largely in the Federal style, this group of early structures form an intimate, powerful quadrangle at the heart of campus. Though now obscured by the colossal east-facing Healy, in the late eighteenth century Old North (1795) was one of the few large-scale structures existing in and around the nation's capital.

The development of these buildings involved great financial struggle, including the Jesuits' significant involvement in American slavery. The central campus emerged under the leadership of multiple Georgetown leaders, beginning with the university's founder, John Carroll, SJ (1735–1815), as well as Georgetown presidents Robert Plunkett, SJ (1791–93); Robert Molyneux, SJ (1793–96 and 1806–8); and Thomas Mulledy, SJ (1829–38 and 1845–48). Mulledy, a leader in the appalling 1838 sale of nearly three hundred enslaved individuals, led the school during the construction of the Infirmary (now Gervase Hall) as well as Isaac Hawkins Hall (which had two previous names). During his presidency, Bernard Maguire, SJ (1852–58 and 1866–70) oversaw the building of his namesake structure, which originally housed the younger students on campus. On the historic core's southern side, Isaac Hawkins Hall, Ryan Hall (occupying the site of the no-longer-extant Old South), and Maguire Hall were and continue to be connected structures, forming a cohesive campus block, with Gervase projecting perpendicularly from the western end of Hawkins.

Developed under the transformative presidency of Patrick Healy, SJ (1873–82), Healy Hall's colossal scale and soaring clock tower serve as a university beacon. Over time, Healy Hall has become an institutional icon. Designed by leading American architects John Smithmeyer (1832–1908) and Paul Pelz (1841–1918), Healy's architecture, despite the use of red brick on its western side, breaks with the earlier Federal mode. A multipurpose structure today, in the late nineteenth century Healy provided much-needed

Restoration of Healy Clock Tower. ca. 1983. (Georgetown University Archives)

new classrooms and science labs, as well as Riggs Library (1891) and Gaston Auditorium (1901).

At the western edge of the quadrangle sits Dahlgren Chapel (1893), a compact Gothic Revival structure completed during the tenure of President J. Havens Richards, SJ (1888–98) through the support of patrons Elizabeth and John Dahlgren (C 1889, L 1891). Over the years the historic core structures have undergone multiple changes and renovations. In 1947 a fire destroyed much of Hawkins Hall, and it was rebuilt with modern materials and a flat roof. Prior to Wolfington Hall opening in 2003, the Jesuits residing on campus lived in Hawkins, Gervase, and Ryan Halls. In the early twenty-first century Ryan and Hawkins were renovated and now serve as undergraduate residences. During the 1980s, Old North underwent an extensive renovation prior to being used by the business school. At the core of the hilltop, this tightly knit brick and granite quadrangle continues to serve as the hub of the university's daily operating needs, including being home to spiritual services, undergraduate housing, administrative offices, class meetings, guest lectures, receptions, and ceremonies.

OPPOSITE: Dahlgren Chapel entrance.

Healy Hall. 1900. (Georgetown University Archives)

Dahlgren Chapel (southwest view).

Old North (1795)

Old North forms the northern arm of the campus's historic core. Originally referred to as simply "the North building," the structure assumed its current name when New North was built adjacent and to the west of it in 1926. Built in 1795, the colossal Old North at that time dwarfed Old South, then the sole other academic building, located just across the yard. Not long after Old South opened, Bishop Carroll sought to enlarge the school's facilities to accommodate expanding enrollment, and in 1794 the land for Old North was purchased from John Threlkeld, a prominent Georgetown citizen and friend of Thomas Jefferson. The brick 154-foot-long Old North possesses a slightly projecting central pavilion capped by a pediment and dormer windows that project from its gable roof. In comparison to the diminutive five-bay (and no longer extant) Old South, Old North extends some seventeen bays in length.

Completed in 1791, Old South possessed Classical central entrances with flanking pilasters, fan lights, and pediments on both the north and south facades. Old South's northern entrance directly faced Old North's entrance with an open courtyard between the two buildings. An early nineteenth-century map drawn by James Curley shows privies on the north and south sides of the historic core. Other buildings, such as a shoe shop and a bakery, were nearby.

On Old North's more elaborate south facade, an arched entranceway and oval window encased in decorative stonework are among the building's ornamental motifs. Also on the south facade are fan windows and prominent keystones above the rectangular windows. Old North's design closely aligns with other early American college architecture, as it emulates Princeton University's Nassau Hall (1756). At the time of its completion, Nassau Hall was the largest building in the English colonies and inspired similar early structures on campuses such as Harvard University, Brown University, and Dartmouth College.

During the nineteenth century, Old North underwent notable exterior changes. To add needed support to the building's north side, two distinctive octagonal towers were added in 1808–10. Around this time builders also added a porch on the south side. Later, in 1866 the northern towers' height was raised roughly 30 feet and adorned with slate roofs and crosses. Coinciding with the construction of Dahlgren Chapel (1893) and the lowering of the quadrangle's courtyard, stairs were added to reach the south entrance. Historian R. Emmett Curran credits Leonard Harbaugh (1749–1822), a Baltimore engineer, with building Old North. Among Harbaugh's noted other commissions are the old Treasury and War Office Buildings in Washington, DC, as well as Trinity Chapel in Georgetown. It is important to note that enslaved individuals also contributed to the construction of this early campus building.

Old North.

Old North first emerged during the terms of Georgetown College presidents Robert Molyneux, SJ (1793–96 and 1806–8) and Louis William DuBourg, SJ (1796–98). Securing the funds to complete Old North's development presented an early challenge for the school's leaders and involved finding multiple revenue sources, including a bank loan; a portion of a scholarship; a donation from past Georgetown president Robert Plunkett, SJ; and earnings from Jesuit plantations where the enslaved labored to support the college. At one point the school offered beef to the builders in lieu of cash. Given these funding challenges, the building's interior remained unfinished until an anonymous gift of $400 in 1808 provided additional monies. At that time, in an effort to complete the flagship structure's interior, even the school's president, William Matthews, SJ (1809), stepped in to help mix mortar.

By the time the Healy Building was completed in 1879, Old North was meeting many needs. It provided needed dormitory space, several classrooms, and a student chapel. The building also housed a museum, a library, the rector's office, and a formal first floor reception area. In 1909 a fire damaged the building's library; a second fire in 1921 led to additional interior renovations.

Over the years many historic figures visited Old North, beginning with George Washington in 1797. Other visitors included the Marquis de Lafayette in 1824, Andrew Jackson in 1831, Ulysses S. Grant in 1869, and Marshall Ferdinand Foch in 1921. In 1814, amid the British attack on Washington, students and faculty watched from the North building as flames ripped through the city.

Mariani & Associates of Washington, DC, led a $6.2 million renovation in 1982–83. At this time the architects added the formal north facade stairway entrance, shifting the focus of Old North away from the enclosed quadrangle. The building's interiors were restored to eighteenth-century Federal style, while builders added steel supporting beams to the roof. Also notable, and highlighted by the *Washington Post* architecture critic at the time, was the innovative steel-and-glass fire stair on the northeast side. The three-story fire stair joins Healy and Old North and distantly echoes the rectangular and circular motifs present in both historic buildings. Also in 1983, on the opposite west side, between Old North and New North, a new brick section with a floor-to-ceiling glass wall was added, housing stairs, elevators, and heating and cooling systems.

During this late twentieth-century renovation the building ceased to be a residence hall. Consequently, Old North now plays a lesser role in student life. Following the restoration, the business school moved into the structure and maximized all available space, including an active student lounge space within its attic story. The McDonough School of Business has since

OPPOSITE: Healy Hall, fire staircase, and Old North.

FDC
OLD NORTH
1795

moved to the modern Rafik B. Hariri Building, and the McCourt School of Public Policy was housed in Old North but is now located downtown, on Georgetown's Capitol Campus. US presidents have continued to visit Old North, including Gerald Ford in 1983, Bill Clinton in 1993, and Barack Obama in 2013.

Gervase Hall (1830)

Located perpendicular to and southwest of Isaac Hawkins Hall, Gervase Hall served as the college's infirmary for many decades. Rooms for sick students occupied the first and second floors until the 1950s, when the building's name changed to Gervase Hall. For many years the Jesuit community occupied the structure, which over time has also housed classrooms, a chapel, a tailor's shop, and a kitchen. Gervase is now used as office space for university administrators.

Although referred to as simply the Infirmary until 1952, at that point the building's name changed to commemorate the Jesuit missionary Thomas Gervase (1590–1637) who, in 1634, traveled from the Isle of Wight in England to St. Mary's County, Maryland, aboard the *Ark*. Nathaniel Marden has been credited with building the structure at a cost of $5,775. Historian Elsa Mendoza notes that Daniel Bussard, a land developer and builder who lived close to campus, hired out four of his enslaved masons for the construction of an early infirmary.

Gervase is a planar brick four-story, six-bay structure. Rectangular and roof dormer windows are among the few features ornamenting the historic structure's simple form. In 1848 the building was widened and a division in the bricks remains visible on the structure's southern end. When Old South was demolished in 1904, builders moved its porch to Gervase Hall's south side. In the late 1920s a four-story addition between Gervase and Isaac Hawkins provided additional infirmary rooms as well as an elevator and a roof garden. In the early 1970s a fire damaged the building, and it remained vacant until being renovated in 1976.

In the late nineteenth century the Infirmary, with window shutters and a small enchanting courtyard garden, projected a welcoming, Victorian environment, which contrasts with the now flat and spare courtyard space and manicured green area and brick walkways leading to Ryan Hall to the east. In 1877 the *Georgetown College Journal* reported that the Infirmary, including its apothecary shop, had grown more ornate through gifts that funded embellishments annually and that the shop even appeared "radiant with pictures, melodious with the singing of canaries, and never without floral decorations." The article described the courtyard as a "delightful pleasure garden" maintained by Jesuits and select students. The picturesque landscape

OPPOSITE: Old North north facade.

Infirmary (later Gervase) exterior, ca. 1900.
(Georgetown University Archives)

Infirmary garden. Photograph by C. M. Bell's Photographic Studio, 1890. (Georgetown University Archives)

contained winding circular paths, bushes, wisteria vines, a small grotto on the north side, and ornaments and vases.

Within Gervase's courtyard stands a statue of Saint Joseph with the Christ Child. An earlier version of the current statue was first placed in the garden in 1872. The intervention and protection of Saint Joseph has been credited with sparing the college from smallpox and measles outbreaks in the city during the early 1870s. Soon thereafter, students created a Saint Joseph Association, which worked to keep a perpetual oil lamp burning near the statue to protect anyone connected with the university from severe illness.

Isaac Hawkins Hall (1832)

Built in 1832 under a different name, this structure now commemorates Isaac Hawkins, one of the 272 enslaved individuals sold by the Jesuits in 1838 and taken from plantations in Maryland to plantations in Louisiana. Hawkins was a sixty-five-year-old man with children, and his name appears at the top of the list of the people who were sold. Prior to 2015 the building memorialized Thomas Mulledy, SJ. Mulledy, an alumnus, served as Georgetown's president from 1829 to 1838 and 1845 to 1848. Along with William McSherry, SJ, Georgetown's president from 1838 to 1839, Mulledy orchestrated the 1838 sale. In 2015 student protests led to removing Mulledy's name and renaming the building Freedom Hall. Two years later, in a ceremony attended by many of the descendants of those sold in 1838, the university rededicated the building and renamed it Isaac Hawkins Hall.

Despite rising student enrollment during Mulledy's presidency, the college faced severe financial challenges during the 1830s, due in part to the building of the Infirmary/Gervase and Isaac Hawkins Halls. By 1838 school administrators had accumulated a debt of over $40,000. An offset to the college's financial woes at this time was Susan Decatur's donation of $7,000. Decatur was the widow of celebrated naval officer Stephen Decatur. After the death of her husband in 1820, she moved to a house near the site of the current White-Gravenor Hall. Despite Decatur's donation, however, the sale of the enslaved individuals became increasingly justified and necessary for the college's financial survival. Moreover, heightened abolitionist sentiment and a depressed economy during the 1830s caused some Jesuits to fear they might lose their enslaved workers without any monetary reward if they did not sell.

Frequently referred to as simply "College Hall" during the nineteenth century, Isaac Hawkins Hall builders Nathaniel Marden and Matthias Duffey have been credited with completing the structure at a cost of roughly $11,000. Like Old North and the Infirmary, it is likely that enslaved labor aided in its construction. The four-story brick building served multiple purposes. A student dining room was on the first floor and a chapel on the

OPPOSITE: Gervase Hall, with Isaac Hawkins Hall to the left and the St. Joseph sculpture in the foreground.

Isaac Hawkins Hall (formerly Mulledy Hall and Freedom Hall), with roof fire damage. Photograph by William C. McHenry, February 1947. (Georgetown University Archives)

second. The third floor housed a large auditorium as well as a study hall. Records from 1947 show that priests had been living in the building's fourth floor rooms when a large fire destroyed a substantial amount of the structure. After this fire, Isaac Hawkins Hall was rebuilt, replacing the building's wooden beams and floors with steel, concrete, and asphalt. A flat roof replaced the earlier pitched roof and dormer windows.

Due to their living quarters' generally poor conditions, the Georgetown Jesuit community moved out of the former Jesuit residences—Isaac Hawkins Hall, Gervase Hall, and Ryan Hall—and moved to Wolfington Hall in 2003. A recent renovation by Ayers Saint Gross has restored Isaac Hawkins Hall for use as an undergraduate student dormitory space.

Ryan Hall

Built in 1904–5 on the site of Old South, Ryan Hall commemorates its patron, Ida M. Ryan (1854–1917), who provided the college with $125,000 for

Ryan Hall.

construction of the building. Born in Baltimore to Roman Catholic parents, Ida Mary Barry married Thomas Fortune Ryan, a successful Wall Street financier. An avid philanthropist, Ida Ryan gave generously to Catholic causes and building projects. Along with funding Ryan Hall, she provided financial support to the construction of Georgetown Hospital as well as Ryan Gymnasium, the latter now part of the Davis Performing Arts Center. Closely connected to the college, four of the Ryans' sons attended Georgetown.

Ryan Hall's elaborate exterior reflects the infusion of European architectural style into Washington, DC, during the late nineteenth century. The building is composed of rich red brick, contrasting cream Indiana limestone and crisp white wood trim. On the south side an imposing two-story Ionic porch rests on a heavy brick arcade. Tall arched windows organize the building's first story, while pilasters and two levels of rectangular windows mark the second and third stories. Above the porch an elaborate white cornice with modillions surrounds the structure. On the building's north and south sides a central dormer window projects from the roof. Brick two-story pilasters mark the building's more austere northern facade.

Architect A. O. Von Herbulis (1861–1928) designed Ryan Hall. Born in Hungary, Von Herbulis practiced in Washington, DC, and designed Holy Cross College (now O'Boyle Hall) at Catholic University. Von Herbulis is also well known for his design of the Cathedral of St. Helena in Helena, Montana. While Ryan Hall's brick exterior melds with the earlier sedate quadrangle buildings, its bold use of the white colonnade and brick arcade echo the Neo-Palladian tradition of Georgian England, as seen in works such as Ernest Flagg's Bourne Residence (1897) in New York. The Second Empire style seen in Washington, DC's Renwick Gallery (1859) and the Eisenhower Executive Office Building (1871–88) may have influenced Ryan Hall's rather elaborate layered composition.

With electricity, new appliances, high ceilings, well-lit spaces and "unrivaled" southern views, Ryan Hall in 1905 was deemed by the *Washington Post* "one of the most up-to-date college buildings of its kind." Nonetheless, others rightly criticized the loss of historic Old South. In 1949 one of Georgetown's past presidents, W. Coleman Nevils, SJ (1878–1955) wrote, "It was an almost unforgivable sin that it [Old South] was razed to make room for that monstrosity, the Ryan Building."

Although now serving as a large multipurpose space, Ryan Hall's first floor was originally a magnificent student dining hall. The room's eight central Ionic pillars and side wall pilasters were covered by a Scaglia finish, providing a marbled appearance. This grand first floor space also served as a dance hall. When the building opened, a modern kitchen with white enamel tiled walls, a bake shop, and a dessert and storage space filled the

Ryan Hall dining hall interior. Photograph by J. Brosnan, SJ, 1906. (Georgetown University Archives)

ground floor below. The building's upper three stories consisted of similarly designed dormitory rooms. Ryan Hall originally housed about fifty-seven students—more than half of the college's total 1904–5 enrollment.

Although originally designed for students, beginning in 1957 the Jesuits lived in Ryan before moving to Wolfington Hall in 2003. Students lived alongside the Jesuits until the mid- to late 1970s, when many students moved out of the building. By 1960 the first-floor dining facility had been relocated to New South. After the Jesuits vacated the building, Ryan Hall sat empty for nearly a decade. In 2013, however, Ryan, along with Isaac Hawkins Hall, underwent a $14.5 million renovation. A primary goal of the project, which received a silver LEED certification, was to provide additional undergraduate student housing on campus. Considering its views over the Potomac River, its restored historic spaces, and its central location, it is now a sought-after undergraduate residential space.

Maguire Hall (1854)

Begun in 1854, Maguire Hall commemorates Bernard Maguire, SJ, who twice served as Georgetown's president, first from 1852 to 1858 and then from 1866 to 1870. Early in his tenure, Maguire separated the younger boys from the older students. To this end, Maguire Hall originally functioned as the Preparatory Building expressly for the younger students. Around 1920 the academy students moved to the Georgetown Preparatory School in Maryland.

Although now tightly sandwiched between Healy Hall to the east and Ryan Hall to the west, the Maguire building once provided a weighty counterbalance to Hawkins Hall, with Old South resting between the two taller brick structures. Echoing Hawkins's earlier profile, chimneys balanced Maguire's east and west ends. Standing five stories including a basement, Maguire possesses a gable roof lined by dormer windows. An arched entranceway on the western corner of the building's south facade and rows of rectangular windows animate the building's compact and otherwise spare exterior.

In the mid-nineteenth century Maguire Hall's basement was used for recreation, the first floor was for dining, the second for study, and the third and fourth as open dormitories. Early in the Civil War soldiers stayed in the building. After the Battles of Bull Run and Antietam, Maguire served as an army hospital. Historian Francis Ballmann notes that, although rejected and never paid, Georgetown sent a $7,500 bill to the government for the use of the buildings during the war.

In the late nineteenth and early twentieth centuries, the Physics Department resided in Maguire Hall. A noted seismograph machine was installed in the

Maguire Hall.

building in 1911. In the 1960s and 1970s, Maguire's first floor served as a library reference room and then as classroom space. In the 1980s much of the building was converted to office use. Today Maguire Hall hosts multiple administrative and other university offices.

Healy Hall (1879)

Healy Hall stands roughly 250 feet west of the university's main O and 37th Streets entrance gates. Designed in a Romanesque Revival style with a rusticated bluish gray stone facade and slate roof, Healy projects a commanding first impression that drastically changed the campus's late nineteenth-century outline when it appeared. In 1878 the *Washington Post* described the then-emerging iconic structure and its site as possessing unsurpassed picturesque American beauty. Designated a National Historic Landmark, Healy Hall is also listed on the National Register of Historic Places.

Healy Hall, which forms the long eastern flank of the campus's U-shaped historic core, stretches over 300 feet north to south and 95 feet east to west. A soaring central clock tower, round arches, gable dormer windows, tall

INTERRELIGIOUS
UNDERSTANDING

Healy Hall.

chimneys, and square corner towers all contribute to Healy's varied profile. A tripartite, four-story structure with an attic and a basement, two north and south end pavilions project from Healy's central mass. The clock tower rises 200 feet, commanding attention from distant points in Virginia and the capital city. In addition to the central tower, a second spire ascends from the structure's southwest corner. Within Healy's central section the arched windows lessen in scale in the upper stories, while the pavilions' windows extend across multiple floors.

Color and materials animate this colossal central campus structure. Sandstone trim, green copper gargoyles, and a smattering of geometrically placed red roof tiles add to the facade's polychromy. Healy's dominant bluestone was quarried near the Potomac River west of Georgetown. In addition to its 3,000 cubic feet of stone, Healy employs over 2 million red bricks. On the building's interior, 300-foot corridors run the length of the building on three floors. Powerful brick arches traverse and support these long halls, while arched wall windows light the passageways. Slightly later, a similar dramatic, large-scale use of brick is seen in Montgomery Meigs's Washington, DC, Pension Bureau Building (1887), now housing the National Building Museum. Along with the stone and brick, some 350,000 feet of Georgia pine was used in Healy Hall's construction.

In contrast to the hall's bold and innovative eastern entry facade, its brick western side blends with the university's earlier adjacent structures. Old North merges with Healy's north wing, and Healy's south wing leads to Maguire Hall. Brick laid in Flemish bond, a central slightly projecting pavilion capped by a stepped gable, two side pavilions, and belt courses between the stories mark Healy's western side.

Excavation for Healy Hall began in 1877, and the building's exterior was finished by 1879. Due to financial constraints, however, Healy's interior remained unfinished for many years. Riggs Library opened in it in 1891, entrance porches were added in 1899, and the Gaston Hall Auditorium interior was not completed until 1901.

The driving vision and determination of President Patrick Healy, SJ, led the building's genesis and construction. The twenty-eighth president of Georgetown, Healy led the school from 1873 to 1882. Born in Georgia, Healy attended the College of the Holy Cross in Massachusetts and later received a PhD from the University of Louvain, Belgium.

Healy Hall's architecture breaks decisively with the college's earlier Federal style brick buildings and sets the stage for the university's increasing national prominence. Moreover, Healy's new orientation—looking toward the city as opposed to toward the Potomac River, like most of the earlier campus buildings—presented a clear shift in the campus's physical layout. This directional change highlighted Georgetown's desire to view itself as an educational institution of national importance.

OPPOSITE: Healy Hall corridor view.

Patrick Healy, SJ (1834–1910).
Photograph by Julius Ulke, 1872.
(Georgetown University Archives)

After deliberation, Healy selected notable Washington architects John L. Smithmeyer (1832–1908) and Paul J. Pelz (1841–1918). The architects carefully studied the site and Smithmeyer designed the original plans and elevations of Healy, while Pelz designed the interior spaces, such as Gaston Hall and Riggs Library, as well as the entrance porches. Born in Vienna, Smithmeyer immigrated to America in 1848. Prior to his Washington, DC, work, he apprenticed in Chicago and then practiced in Indianapolis. Pelz, originally from Prussia, came to the United States in 1851. He later worked in New York City as a draftsman for architect Detlef Lienau. Prior to joining forces with Smithmeyer in 1872, Pelz worked as a civil engineer and architect for the US Lighthouse Board in Washington, DC. Before winning the Healy Hall commission, in 1873 Smithmeyer and Pelz won the competition for Washington's celebrated Library of Congress building. The development of the library was a long, embattled political process and ultimately work on it did not begin until 1886.

In the late nineteenth century, American architects appropriated a myriad of European architectural styles, and Smithmeyer and Pelz were no exception. Healy's Romanesque Revival architectural style—marked by its rounded arches and weighty mass—creates an aura of a European past rich in culture. The Romanesque Revival mode was prevalent in numerous sites across America at the time. In the late 1870s, leading architect Henry Hobson Richardson (1838–86) used a more controlled Romanesque Revival style at Harvard University and elsewhere. Architect Richard Upjohn's earlier Bowdoin College Chapel (1855) preceded Healy's use of rusticated stone, rounded arches, and bifora windows. Healy Hall certainly reflects the eclecticism that marks late nineteenth-century American architecture, and its pointed arches, vertical thrust, and gargoyles also align with the Gothic Revival. Healy's time studying abroad would have exposed him to northern European architectural precedents, and the stepped gables apparent on Healy Hall's western side echo not only Sir G. G. Scott's St. Pancras Station in London (1868–74) but northern European building traditions as well.

Despite its bold form and cosmopolitan style, funding Healy Hall's completion proved to be an enormous challenge for President Healy. The building eventually cost $300,000, and the initial loan for construction proved inadequate. Healy sought donations from several prominent alumni, such as W. W. Corcoran, the founder of the Corcoran Gallery of Art, and ultimately even the Jesuits' food and clothing budgets were tapped to help finance the structure's completion. A writer for the April 1879 *College Journal* implored readers to fund the completion of Healy's interior spaces, noting that "hundreds of thousands of dollars have been showered upon . . . other colleges, yet Georgetown, the peer of them all, the alma mater even of millionaires, has been left to fight its battle *alone* in this 'gilded age' of the 'mighty dollar.'"

Healy Hall has always functioned as a multipurpose structure, and in the late nineteenth century it met the college's need for additional classrooms, science laboratories, and an auditorium. Originally Healy's basement contained a chemistry laboratory and lecture room. The first floor entrance, originally dedicated to students and located beneath the clock tower, continues to divide classrooms on either side. Similar in layout to the first, Healy's second and third floors originally served as dormitory spaces. Along with the Office of the President, various institutional and academic offices currently reside within the building. The historic Philodemic Hall remains within its north pavilion and is currently undergoing renovation and reenvisioning. For more than forty years, between 1889 and 1931, the northern pavilion's Coleman Museum, named for its benefactor, James V. Coleman, housed a collection of coins, medals, and natural history objects.

RIGGS MEMORIAL LIBRARY

Completed in 1891 and designed by Pelz, Riggs Memorial Library functioned as the college library until Lauinger Library opened in 1970. Donations given by E. Francis Riggs of the Washington Riggs Bank as a memorial to his father and brother, provided over $10,000 toward the library's construction costs.

Situated within Healy Hall's south pavilion, Riggs Memorial Library is one of only a few remaining libraries in the United States built of cast iron. The library possesses a central reading room surrounded by three levels of open cast-iron book stacks, with the upper stories accessed via winding staircases. A pioneer for its time, a skylight covers Riggs's central space and multifloor windows cast abundant natural light throughout the library. In 1889 Pelz noted of the reading room's design that all obstructions to the light, by floors and interior stairwells, were "carefully avoided."

Each floor of the library is slightly over 7 feet tall, to allow the shelved books to be accessed without a ladder. The cast-iron columns, stairs, and shelves were prefabricated and numbered for assembly on-site. Elaborate iron foliate designs also decorate the library's radiators.

After Lauinger took over as the university's primary library, the Fine Arts Department occupied Riggs during the later 1970s. A 1982 renovation, led by EPR Inc. and lauded by the American Institute of Architects, restored the library's Victorian color and grandeur. While it continues to serve its original purpose of housing books, Riggs Library is now used largely for special events and receptions.

OPPOSITE: Riggs Library interior. Copyright © 1983 Walter Smalling Jr. (Georgetown University Archives)

GASTON HALL AUDITORIUM

Gaston Hall Auditorium, with a seating capacity of roughly seven hundred, was named for the school's first student, William B. Gaston. Completed in 1901, Gaston Hall occupies the upper floors of Healy Hall's northern pavilion. A U-shaped balcony with seating below provides multiple views of the auditorium's stage.

In 1900 the university commissioned Br. Francis Schroen, SJ, to design the hall's interior decoration. The interior employs Renaissance-inspired decorative motifs and allegorical paintings. Displaying elements of the broader American Renaissance movement, the earlier Library of Congress building interior mural decoration provided an important general precedent for Schroen's design. Within the auditorium, crests of Catholic colleges and universities fill the arches under the cornice. At the rear of the stage are plaques with the names of scholars and scientists and emblems of their respective field (microscope, books, etc.). Two prominent allegorical paintings hang above and behind the stage: To the south is enthroned Faith with Morality and Patriotism to her right and left; to the north the painting depicts Alma Mater giving victory wreaths to Art and Science. Figures of Athena and a classically dressed athlete flank the two scenes on the right and left. Richly hued stained glass windows and large wooden ceiling coffers further add to Gaston Hall's ornate interior.

Gaston Hall interior. Photograph by J. Brosnan, SJ. (Georgetown University Archives)

Dahlgren Chapel (1893)

Begun in 1892 and originally referred to as the Chapel of the Sacred Heart, Dahlgren Chapel sits within the campus's historic core. Facing east and nestled behind Healy Hall, this pristine, compact Gothic Revival structure is surrounded by the university's oldest buildings. Old North and New North flank one side and Gervase/Isaac Hawkins Halls plus Ryan and Maguire Halls line the quadrangle's south side. The chapel's distinct form emulates English Gothic structures of the thirteenth century. James Renwick Jr.'s Oak Hill Cemetery Chapel in Georgetown (1850) provides a notable nearby Gothic Revival precedent. The campus's first structure dedicated to worship, Dahlgren Chapel, consecrated in 1893, was also the earliest university building to be funded entirely through outside gifts.

Elizabeth Drexel Dahlgren and her husband, John Vinton Dahlgren (C 1889, L 1891), provided the funding for construction of the chapel, which was designed as a memorial to their first child, Joseph Drexel Dahlgren. Joseph died of pneumonia at the age of sixteen months, and along with those of other Dahlgren family members, his body is interred in the chapel's crypt. Members of the social elite, the Dahlgrens lived in New York City, where John worked as an attorney. Over the course of the chapel's construction and decoration, the Dahlgrens grew close to then-president of Georgetown J. Havens Richards, SJ. Richards was instrumental in convincing the Dahlgrens to fund the structure.

Cruciform in plan, Dahlgren Chapel extends some 100 feet in length and 40 feet in width, with robust transepts on its north and south sides. The building rises to a height of just over 60 feet. Built of red brick and designed to originally seat 350 people, Dahlgren possesses a gray slate gable roof crowned by a bell cot at its eastern entrance. The chapel's bell, originally cast in 1814 for the Calvert Mansion in Riverdale, Maryland, was installed in the early 1890s. Contrasting with the structure's rich red brick, light tan Indiana limestone trim surrounds the chapel's entranceway, windows, bell tower, and other accents. A prominent rose window adorns the east entrance porch. Set inside a lunette with corner quatrefoils, thick tracery in the form of a cross marks the central rose window. Tall lancet windows pierce the building's exterior walls, while buttresses provide exterior support.

Henry Simpson, of the architectural firm Barry & Simpson, designed Dahlgren Chapel, while John S. Larcombe built the structure. In 1892 a writer for the *Georgetown College Journal* described Simpson as "an English Catholic, who obtained his knowledge of church architecture from the pure models of ancient English abbeys, monasteries and churches." The *Journal* reporter further observed that Mr. Simpson had "fallen in perfect accord with the wishes of Mrs. Dahlgren" and "produced a design simple yet elegant, with a loyalty to the standards of pure gothic."

OPPOSITE: Dahlgren Chapel exterior.

Along with details at the entrance and its window tracery and dormer windows, also notable among Dahlgren's exterior ornament is a lone, adeptly carved scholarly monk on the chapel's northwest side. Created by James F. Earley, this endearing hooded figure rests near the roofline, intently reading a folio. Earley, who arrived from Europe to the nation's capital in the 1880s, was the father of the noted Washington artisan and sculptor John J. Earley. The younger Earley completed significant work in the city, including an innovative concrete surface cover at Meridian Hill Park. Before carving the monk, the senior Earley asked Richards for permission to proceed. Surprisingly, Earley is believed to have completed the monk in just a few hours. The sculptor's efforts paid off, as Earley later received the contract to carve the chapel's intricate interior nave capitals, which depict grapes and other decorative foliage.

In the 1890s the *College Journal* described the chapel's interior as "even more chaste and tasteful" than its exterior. Inside, a timber roof covers Dahlgren's nave and chancel area. Three pointed arches separate the transepts from the nave on both the north and south sides. Along with the rich wood and distinctive archways, vibrantly hued stained glass windows animate Dahlgren's intimate interior. Under Elizabeth's and John Dahlgren's watchful eyes, Mayer & Company of Munich, Germany, and New York designed nearly all the chapel's stained glass windows. The altar window depicts the Holy Family flanked by Saint Elizabeth of Hungary and Saint John the Evangelist, the Dahlgrens' patron saints. Above these figures rests the Society of Jesus monogram (IHS). Margaret Mary Alacoque and Claude de la Columbière, both associated with devotion to the Sacred Heart, reside within flanking quatrefoils. Transept windows depict Holy Communion and Saint John the Evangelist to the north and Saint Elizabeth of Hungary's virtues of charity, humility, and victory to the south. A vibrant rose window dominates the chapel's eastern side. In the later 1890s, windows were added to the nave, depicting Saint Thomas More, Saint Helena, and Saint Ignatius of Loyola on the south side and to the north Saint Louis of France, Saint Joan of Arc, and Saint Aloysius Gonzaga. Bronze depictions of the Stations of the Cross rest between the windows, their dark hue contrasting with the nave's white walls. In the 1990s depictions of John Henry Newman and Saint Isaac Jogues were added to the windows on either side of the chapel's main entrance.

Over the course of its more than 125-year life, Dahlgren Chapel has undergone several important renovations. Funded by gifts to the university by the Dahlgrens' second son, John Dahlgren Jr., the first renovation occurred in the mid-twentieth century. At this time, among other changes, the ivy that covered much of the structure was removed. The most controversial chapel restoration, however, occurred in the 1970s, when the Second Vatican Council impacted the desire to transform the structure's interior. Notable

OPPOSITE: Dahlgren Chapel. Photograph by Art Jerome, 1952. (Georgetown University Archives)

Dahlgren Chapel stone monk. Photograph by John Brosnan, SJ, 1916. (Georgetown University Archives)

was the council's requirement of active congregation participation in the liturgy. Campus Ministries director Rev. Lawrence Madden, SJ, was a key proponent of the transformation, although he faced significant campus opposition. In 1974 *The Hoya* newspaper labeled the opposing sides of the Dahlgren renovation debate the "revisionists" versus the "ritualists." Thomas M. King, SJ, assistant professor of theology, aligned with the latter group and argued that changes would bring "flexibility" to Dahlgren's interior space at the expense of its "personality." Ultimately included among the changes that were completed in 1976 were the replacement of pews with movable chairs, the creation of a more level floor to facilitate multipurpose use of the space, the installation of a new oak altar in the sanctuary center, and the removal of the traditional style overhead hanging lights. Much later improvements continued with significant renovations taking place in 1989 and 2014. The latter restoration, which included structural reinforcement, stained glass restoration, and new seating, as well as sound and lighting enhancements, was made possible by a financial gift from Francis (C 1975, L 1978) and Kathleen (SFS 1977) Rooney and others. Despite its diminutive stature, Dahlgren Chapel continues to serve as a spiritual stronghold within the Georgetown campus core, holding daily Masses and special services throughout the year.

Dahlgren Chapel interior.

Dahlgren Chapel interior. Photograph by John Brosnan, SJ, 1916. (Georgetown University Archives)

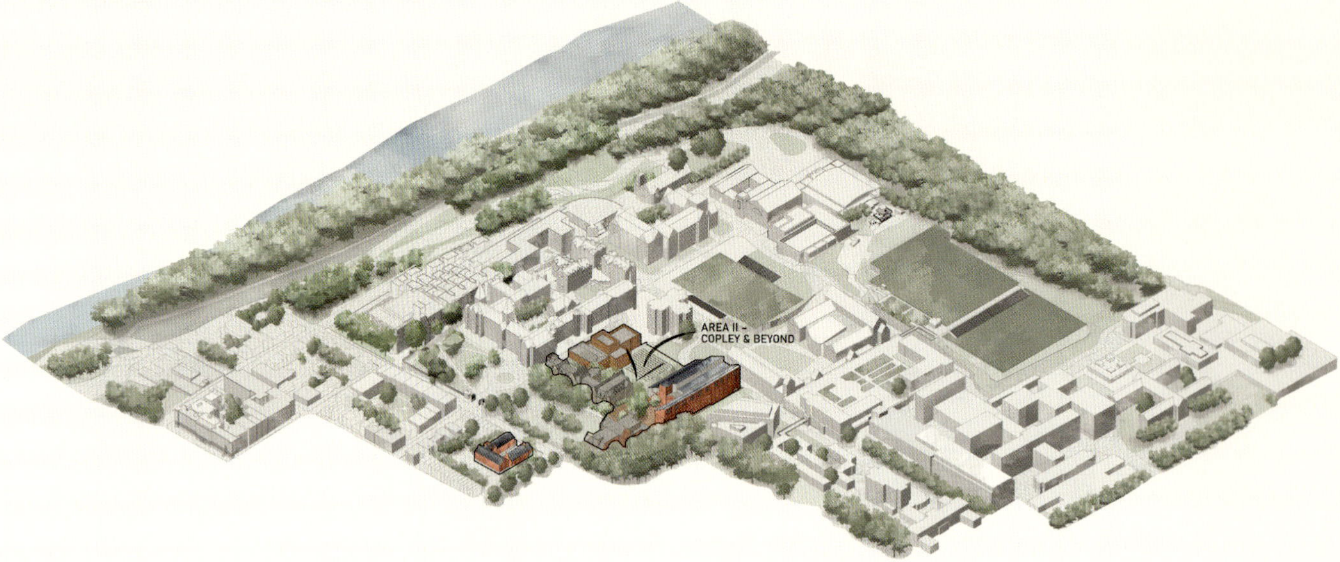
AREA II –
COPLEY & BEYOND

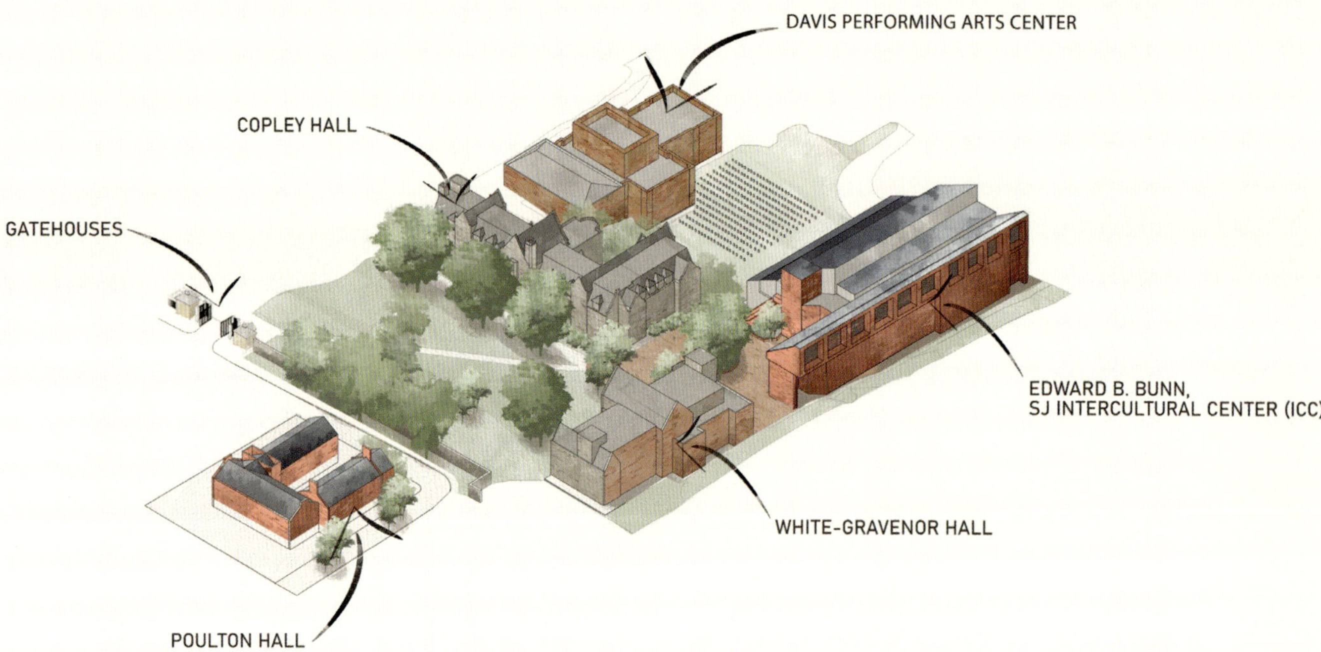
DAVIS PERFORMING ARTS CENTER
COPLEY HALL
GATEHOUSES
EDWARD B. BUNN,
SJ INTERCULTURAL CENTER (ICC)
WHITE-GRAVENOR HALL
POULTON HALL

Copley and Beyond

A review of Area II begins with the mid-nineteenth-century gatehouses that mark the main entrance to the campus at 37th and O Streets. Poulton Hall (1947) resides just outside the gatehouses along 37th Street and exemplifies the campus's historic ties to the World War II era. Just inside the entrance gates, Copley Hall (1932) and its lawn, as well as White-Gravenor Hall (1933), which currently houses the Admissions Office, welcome the visitor to campus. Architect Emile G. Perrot designed the Collegiate Gothic–style Copley and White-Gravenor Halls during W. Coleman Nevils's Depression-era tenure. In the nineteenth century, prior to the development of Copley Hall and White-Gravenor Hall, an athletic field occupied the Copley entrance lawn, while the home of Susan Decatur (1776–1860), the widow of naval commander Stephen Decatur, was situated where White-Gravenor Hall now stands. Susan Decatur, a school benefactor, had converted to Catholicism in the early nineteenth century.

The centrally located Davis Performing Arts Center first emerged in the early twentieth century. This originally compact brick structure has had multiple functions throughout its life: beginning as the Ryan Gymnasium (1906–52), then serving as an administration center (1952–2005), and finally the current theater and performing arts center (2005–present). In the first half of the twentieth century, Georgetown's basketball team practiced at Ryan, prior to the opening of McDonough Gymnasium in the southwest area of campus.

Criticized by some, the angular modern Edward B. Bunn, SJ Intercultural Center (ICC) certainly contrasts with the historical style of Copley and White-Gravenor Halls. The ICC opened in 1982 and is home to the School of Foreign Service as well as numerous departments across the humanities and social sciences. The ICC was a pioneering structure, not only for its global purpose but also for its colossal array of rooftop solar panels. Fronting the ICC is the Red Square Courtyard. This flexible campus throughway provides an area for student gatherings, protests, and various celebrations such as art fairs and food events.

Poulton Hall. Photograph by Kramer-Boduie, 1950.
(Georgetown University Archives)

Entrance gatehouse with Healy Hall in the background.

Copley lawn with Healy Hall in the distance.

Gatehouses (Mid-Nineteenth Century)

The squat and stalwart north and south Gatehouses flank the main 37th and O Street campus entrance. Essentially square in form, both Gatehouses possess a hipped roof and central chimney. The Gatehouses date to the mid-nineteenth century and have served a variety of unique functions over time.

During the 1850s the north Gatehouse operated as an armory for the Georgetown College Cadets, a voluntary military group of students on campus. In 1861, when Union soldiers were stationed on campus, the north Gatehouse was used as a jail for individuals who had committed minor criminal offenses. Later, in 1876, the *Georgetown College Journal* reported that one long-term employee of the campus shoe shop kept a room within one of the Gatehouses. In the early nineteenth century, a campus shoemaker shop was located just west of Old North.

During the twentieth century the Gatehouses changed physically and once again took on varied roles. The structures were remodeled around 1913, with rough-hewn stone replacing the earlier brick construction and a single eastern window taking the place of two existing shuttered windows. During the mid-1950s the Gatehouses were moved further apart to create a larger automobile-friendly entrance. At the time, *The Hoya* commented that this

Main entrance Gatehouse.

Georgetown University, Washington, D.C., The College Gate. Postcard ca. 1910. (Georgetown University Archives)

new entrance replaced the "archaic and out-moded carriage width gate" and now permitted "at least two Cadillacs at a time to enter" campus. During the 1960s the Gatehouses served as a student-operated gift shop and information booth associated with the college bookstore. Later, during the 1980s, the north Gatehouse served as a ticket office for the Georgetown University Transportation Service, which later moved to the Leavey Student Center. The south Gatehouse has often served as a campus visitor information booth.

Poulton Hall (1947)

Poulton Hall commemorates Ferdinand Poulton, SJ, a founder of the American Jesuit community who arrived in Maryland in 1638. President W. Coleman Nevils, SJ, originally planned to erect a structure commemorating Poulton that would rest immediately perpendicular to White-Gravenor Hall and form the eastern side of a grand U-shaped quadrangle, all in the august Collegiate Gothic style. The economic woes of the Depression, however, interfered with the completion of Nevils's plan.

Instead, the current Poulton Hall is actually a surplus World War II government building. Its two long gable-roofed structures were originally part of a large chemical explosives manufacturing plant located at the Susquehanna subdepot near Williamsport, Pennsylvania. During the war the site functioned as a filler depot for overseas armament shipments. After the war, the Lanham Act authorized the Federal Works Agency to transfer surplus military buildings to institutions that needed to augment their academic facilities for the education of returning veterans. Georgetown University,

Poulton Hall.

along with five Pennsylvania universities, received buildings from the war manufacturing plant.

In 1947 two wooden structures were transported from the plant to the university. They were later joined into one structure and encased in brick. Unobstructed by columns, Poulton Hall's large classrooms were able to accommodate over two hundred students. This was key in the post–World War II era, when, like many colleges across the country, Georgetown's enrollment surged. The GI Bill subsidized and provided an education stipend to any veteran, and Georgetown experienced phenomenal enrollment increases, in large part due to the influx of these veterans. Historian R. Emmett Curran notes that of the nearly twenty-six hundred students at Georgetown in 1946, 52 percent were veterans, nearly all of them attending courtesy of the GI Bill. In 1944 the aggregate enrollment in the university was about sixteen hundred; by 1948 enrollment had surged to nearly six thousand.

Poulton Hall originally housed both classroom spaces and the college bookstore. However, it was the structure's innovative electronic language lab that made news in 1950. The *Washington Post* reported, "The world's most modern system of language teaching—by electronics—was formally introduced . . . into the curriculum at Georgetown University," with an accompanying image of row upon row of students in the Poulton lab, each equipped with a headset. Poulton Hall currently houses multiple university units, including Health Education Services, the Department of Arabic and Islamic Studies, the Center for Social Justice, the Mask and Bauble Dramatic Society, the Performing Arts Department faculty offices, and the Department of Linguistics.

Classrooms from a TNT Building

One of the new large classrooms which seats 218 and has no obstructing columns.

The TNT plant before it was dismantled. The wing at the far left is the one now at Georgetown. Five Pennsylvania schools also obtained sections of the building. *Federal Works Agency Photos.*

"Classrooms from a TNT Building" newspaper clipping. Federal Works Agency Photos, (Georgetown University Archives)

"Students in 'Language Lab' at Georgetown." Poulton Language Lab, *Washington Post*, November 22, 1950. The caption reads: "In semi-soundproof booths, students, with earphones, learn foreign tongues by electronics."

Copley Hall (1932)

Designed by architect Emile G. Perrot, Copley Hall commands a linchpin campus spot just north of Healy Hall. Clearly visible from the 37th and O Street entrance gates, Copley forms the western arm of the main campus quadrangle. Now facing Copley lawn, the hall was the first structure to emerge within the quadrangle, replacing the earlier athletic field. Copley Hall opened in 1932 and continues to serve as a student dormitory, housing roughly three hundred students every year. This Depression-era building commemorates Thomas Copley, SJ (1596–1652), a prominent Jesuit who arrived in Maryland in 1636.

Designed in the Collegiate Gothic style, Copley's long rectangular form is anchored by a large central pavilion capped by a gable roof. Smaller pavilions reside on the north and south sides of the building, while dormer windows and an off-center bell tower further animate the building's roofline. Copley's variegated gray granite is accented by a golden-brown stone, while the light limestone trim provides a contrast to the building's overall presentation. Additional supporting stone came from an old M Street bridge over Rock Creek that was dismantled in 1929. Aiming to complement yet not overshadow Healy Hall, the building was simplified in its design process. An early Perrot drawing shows somewhat more elaborate side oriel windows and a more symmetrical composition than the final structure contains. Copley's stepped gable roof motif also echoes Healy Hall's western roofline. Despite choosing the Collegiate Gothic style, Perrot employed structural steel beams and concrete fireproof floors. In 1931 the most up-to-date fire alarm signal bell and telephone systems were installed on all floors. The dormitory rises five stories, with a large formal lounge on the first floor of the north wing.

Early drawing for Copley Hall. Emile G. Perrot, ca. 1928. (Georgetown University Archives)

Copley Hall entrance.

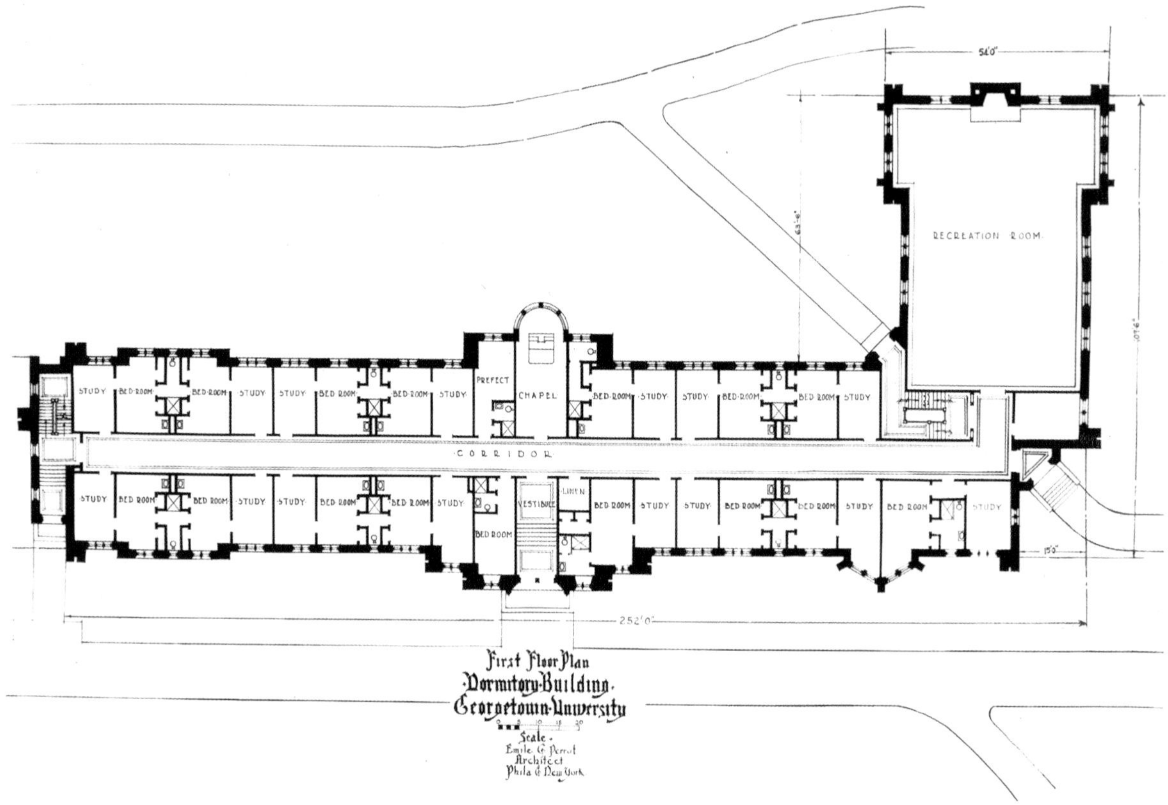

Copley Hall First Floor Plan. Emile G. Perrot, ca. 1929. (Georgetown University Archives)

As with the slightly later-constructed White-Gravenor Hall to the north, Copley emerged under the micromanagement of W. Coleman Nevils. Most of Copley Hall has suites with two double rooms and a bathroom. Nevils was adamant about the incorporation of private bathrooms in the design of the suites, countering what he perceived as uncivilized communal lavatories.

Like White-Gravenor, Copley Hall's exterior possesses a myriad of ornament linking the structure to the university's heritage and Jesuit tradition. Among its many decorations is a large Latin inscription on the middle gable, which reads: "Moribus Antiquis Res Stat Loyolaea Virisque." The *College Journal* in 1933 translated the motto as, "Loyola's Fortune Still May Hope to Thrive, If Men and Mold like Those of Old Survive." Flanking the entrance door the dates of 1634 and 1789 are inscribed, as well as a shield on each side, one referencing the first Mass conducted by the early Jesuits in Maryland and the other acknowledging university founder John Carroll. Above the main entrance door is a prominent three-story oriel window. Four shields between the windows represent extracurricular activities important to the early college: the Sodality, or Christian brotherhood; athletics; the Philodemic (debating) Society; and a written journal.

The north bay window of Copley Hall commemorates past Georgetown students who went on to become leaders in their fields. An article in

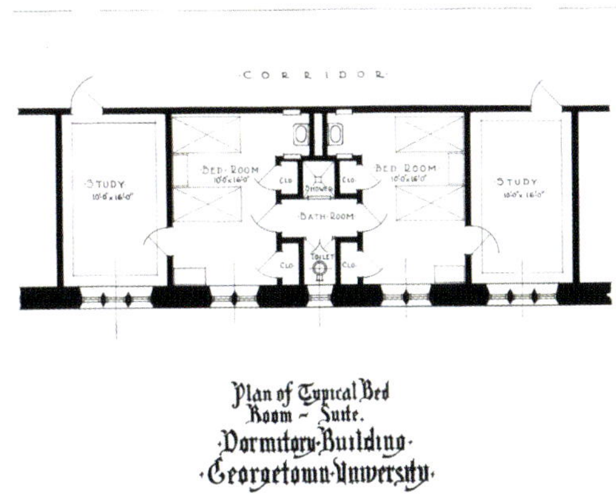

Copley Hall Suite Plan. Emile G. Perrot, ca. 1929. (Georgetown University Archives)

Copley Hall south tower.

the 1933 *Georgetown College Journal* notes the following fields and individuals: Edward D. White/Justice; William Gaston/Law; James R. Randall/Poetry; William W. Corcoran/Art; Henry P. Northrop/Church; Edwin Kavanagh/State; Benjamin A. Young/Theology; Colonel Julius P. Garesche/Army; Charles Boarman Jr./Navy; Robert Walsh/Prose; Thomas Herran/ Diplomacy; and Salvator Tongiorgi/Philosophy. Copley Hall's south tower features the family crest of the Jesuits' founder, Saint Ignatius of Loyola; the seal of the University of Paris, where Ignatius was educated; and the seal of the Society of Jesus.

Copley Hall also houses two important chapels. Opposite the main entrance on the first floor is the Servant of God Sister Thea Bowman Chapel of Saint William. This chapel commemorates Thea Bowman (1937–90), a black Catholic nun and racial justice advocate. Until 2022 the chapel's name memorialized William Cowardin, SJ (1849–1925), a past Georgetown University professor and chaplain. During the Civil War Cowardin fought as a member of the Confederate Army. Originally constructed to be the

Copley Hall and chapel under construction, ca. 1930. (Georgetown University Archives)

"seniors' chapel," the aim was to provide to the students living in Copley an opportunity to deepen their faith during their final educational year. The stained glass windows within the chapel depict the parables of Jesus as well as subjects from the book of Daniel, in honor of Daniel McFadden, SJ.

Also within Copley's west wing and directly under the Bowman Chapel of Saint William is the Crypt Chapel. This chapel was originally dedicated to eight seventeenth-century French Jesuit missionaries who settled in Ontario, Canada, among the Indigenous Huron people. The chapel's stained glass windows highlight the Jesuit missionaries, now considered martyrs. Heavy ribbed vaults and solid stout piers support this diminutive campus sacred space. Historically, wakes for deceased Jesuits were held here prior to burial the next morning in the nearby Jesuit Community Cemetery. Today, Orthodox Christian liturgical services are held here. Recently restored, the Crypt Chapel also includes a series of vibrant painted icons.

—SR & GR

White-Gravenor Hall (1933)

Designed by Emile G. Perrot under the auspices of W. Coleman Nevils, White-Gravenor Hall marks the north end of the campus's entry quadrangle and continues the Collegiate Gothic style of Copley Hall to its west. The building was named for Andrew White, SJ (1579–1656) and John Gravenor, SJ (1589–1640). Both Jesuits were among the 140 English men and women aboard the *Ark* and the *Dove,* which arrived in southern Maryland in the 1630s.

As with Copley Hall, when designing White-Gravenor Hall, Perrot aimed to create a structure that would blend harmoniously with the "unsurpassed" Healy Hall. The five-part White-Gravenor is composed of a central projecting pavilion, extensions, two side anchor pavilions, a flat, crenelated western roof, and a pointed gable on the eastern pavilion. A long rectangular esplanade fronts the building, while a ten-foot cross caps the central pavilion, below which is inscribed the Georgetown seal. The inscription Ad Maiorem Dei Gloriam, translated as "For the Greater Glory of God," appears at the base of the central pavilion's gable. The building's blue-gray granite stone, taken from the same Maryland quarry used for the construction of Copley Hall, is sprinkled amid the contrasting golden brown locally quarried granite stone.

White-Gravenor Hall.

White-Gravenor Hall entrance detail. Photograph by John Brosnan, SJ, 1935. (Georgetown University Archives)

During the height of the Great Depression, the erection of White-Gravenor Hall provided key jobs for otherwise unemployed construction workers. In 1933 this was one of the largest construction jobs in the district, and the *Washington Star* reported that White-Gravenor was one of the earliest DC buildings to respond to President Herbert Hoover's call for emergency construction work to aid the unemployed.

The architects expressly designed White-Gravenor Hall to accommodate the Chemistry Department, providing important new labs, classrooms, and spacious lecture halls. In addition, White-Gravenor's basement originally housed a large cafeteria. When it first opened, the press praised the building's windows, modern ventilation system, and thermostat-controlled heating system. Ever the micromanager, Nevils was even involved in the selection of the furniture details, demanding that the chairs, desks, and laboratory tables all be engraved with the Georgetown University seal. More recently, along with continuing to provide needed classroom spaces, White-Gravenor Hall houses the Office of the Registrar along with the Admissions Office.

White-Gravenor Hall has been deemed a "sermon in stone," with its ornament connecting the building to the Jesuit order's early history in Maryland as well as the university's early years. Within the spandrels flanking the pointed entrance arch are two shields. The western shield commemorates the early Maryland Jesuits, with images of the *Ark* as well as symbols of the first Mass conducted in Maryland—a church bell, a chalice, and a tree under which the liturgy was celebrated. The eastern shield shows John Carroll's coat of arms. In the early nineteenth century, Jesuit Jonathan West donated considerable central campus land to the university, and his name presides over the building's western entrance. West also laid out the campus's early Walks, a serpentine nineteenth-century wooded path that stretched northward from White-Gravenor Hall's later site and looped back toward Old North. Directly above the White-Gravenor central entrance are four shields symbolizing academies founded by the Jesuits in Maryland as well as a fifth for Georgetown: 1634 St. Mary's City; 1640 Calverton Manor; 1677 Newtown Manor; 1745 Bohemia Manor; and 1789 Georgetown Heights.

The three-story oriel over the main entrance includes carved shields, each with a symbol representing an academic subject accompanied by the name of a Jesuit educator prominent in that field. For example, the lamp of learning with the image of Francisco Suárez represents philosophy; lab instruments

White-Gravenor Hall under construction, ca. 1933. (Georgetown University Archives)

with the image of Athanasius Kircher represent science. Other subjects and educators included among the second-floor seals are poetry (Maciej Kazimierz Sarbievius), Greek (Jacob Gretser), English (Robert Southwell), math (Christopher Clavius), and history (Johannes Bollandus). Similarly, the third floor seals represent various elective courses: French tragedy (Georges Longhaye), Italian oratory (Paolo Segneri), Spanish satire (José Francisco de Isla), German literary criticism (Alexander Baumgartner), economics (Juan de Mariana), education (Joseph Jouvency), and military science (James Clark).

Amid its many symbols and images, White-Gravenor Hall's sermon in stone imagery also highlights the university's sordid relationship with slavery. Above the left entrance is a crest memorializing Br. Joseph Mobberly, SJ, an overseer at Maryland's Saint Inigoes manor plantation, who later taught at Georgetown. In the 1820s, amid rising arguments for abolishing slavery, Mobberly continued to justify the institution, using racist ideology that people of African descent are inferior. The treatment of the enslaved at the plantation was brutal, and Mobberly was dismissed due to conduct complaints.

Ryan Gymnasium (1906)/Administration Building/ Davis Performing Arts Center

The building that currently houses the Davis Performing Arts Center, formerly the Ryan Gymnasium, has served three distinct functions since its initial construction in 1906: as an athletic gymnasium (1906–52), as an administration center (1952–2005), and as a performing arts center (2005–present). While the purpose of the building and its interior have changed dramatically over the course of its lifetime, the brick exterior and signature double-height arched windows have remained intact (albeit modernized) and preserve the structure's historical identity.

The architectural firm Ewing & Chappell of New York designed the original building, with John Larcombe serving as the builder. Funding for the original structure came from university patron Ida M. Ryan of New York, who also sponsored Ryan Hall. The 1906 rectangular structure's fenestration is striking. Four large, double-height arched windows on the parallel longer sides provide ample natural light in the interior, while another two identical windows anchor the structure's short ends. The window arches are accentuated by a brick header and keystones. Moreover, a large skylight spanning the entire length of the hipped roof lets in even more natural light. The main entrance is ornamented by a gable in the roofline flanked by pilasters.

When Ryan served as a gymnasium, the walls were exposed brick with wood-paneled wainscoting below the windows, and exposed bolted metal

Gonda Theatre entrance, Davis Performing Arts Center.

Ryan Administration Building, 1960. (Georgetown University Archives)

Ryan Gymnasium interior. Photograph by John Brosnan, SJ, 1910. (Georgetown University Archives)

trusses supported the roof. Electric light bulbs hung from the rafters surrounded by metal cages for protection against stray basketballs. An elevated track balcony projected from the gym's perimeter above the wooden floor. The gymnasium was originally designed to serve some 250 students, and in its day it adequately met the school's needs. The building also provided an important foundation for the growth of Georgetown's basketball team during the first half of the twentieth century. It did not, however, also have room for spectators, and by the mid to late 1920s, with the completion of New North (fostering enrollment growth to close to a thousand students), Ryan Gymnasium was believed to be inadequate. Before the opening of McDonough Gymnasium in 1952, Ryan Gymnasium underwent interior alterations to improve the facility. For example, in 1940 the elevated track was removed, and for good reason, as it interfered with shots from the corner of the basketball court.

Despite the limitations of the old gym, one of the most beloved features was its trophy room, which showcased the university's athletes. The *Georgetown College Journal* described the trophy room's "very attractive appearance" and provided details of the space, with taxidermy deer heads mounted on the wall above pictures of athletic teams dating back to 1889.

After the construction of McDonough Gym, Ryan Gymnasium was converted to an administrative center. The *Georgetown Record* detailed the planned transformation from gym to university administrative "nerve center":

> Occupying the lower floor of the building will be a centralized University Records department. The main, or present playing floor will be taken over by the Treasurer's Office, including the accounting branches and the Bursar's functions. Another floor, to be added under the present roof, will provide space for the offices of University Development, Public Relations and University Placement. The Administration Building will house an interior-dial telephone control board. In the lobby a receptionist will greet campus visitors and maintain an information bureau.

These changes occurred primarily on the building's interior; the exterior remained largely untouched until the early 2000s, when the building's purpose changed yet again. In 2005 the building was added to and converted into the Davis Performing Arts Center. The Davis Center addition is the campus's first structure built expressly for the performing arts. Dedicated to Royden B. Davis, a Jesuit priest who was dean of Georgetown College from 1966 to 1989, the conversion and addition cost over $30 million to complete. The MBNA Corporation was a major donor for the project.

Nationally recognized architect Hugh Hardy (1932–2017) transformed and greatly expanded the Ryan Gymnasium to the west of the original structure. Celebrated for his theater designs, Hardy restored several New

Davis Performing Arts Center, beyond the Jesuit Community Cemetery.

York City landmarks and public spaces, including Radio City Music Hall and the New Amsterdam Theatre. Hardy designed many other performing arts and cultural venues as well, such as New York's New Victory Theater. Within the Davis Center, the old gym area now serves as the entrance and lobby to the performing arts center, which includes the 239-seat Gonda Theatre, the black box Devine Studio Theatre, classrooms, and theater production learning laboratories. The original wood-frame windows were replaced with metal ones, and the main entrance was shifted to the narrower southern facade with an added glass canopy. The addition's protruding brick attic houses the fly-space for lighting and scenery above the Gonda Theatre's stage.

Washington Post architecture critic Benjamin Forgey lambasted the Davis Center's exterior for its failure to convey theatrical pizzazz. Interestingly, Hardy originally designed a more decorative exterior of geometric patterns of light and dark brick. However, the project's patron, Los Angeles businessman Lou Gonda, wanted a more conservative structure. As Forgey noted, "When you hire an architect of Hardy's caliber and experience, the best idea is simply to let him follow his own instincts." Despite the rather lackluster brick shell, the addition's interior theater space is effective and vibrant. The lobby contains exposed ductwork, which echoes the steel trusses of the old gym. An intimate theater space, the Gonda Theatre possesses strong acoustics and brightly patterned seating.

The Ryan Gymnasium building, in all three iterations, has served a vital role to Georgetown University: from its origins as the gymnasium, which served as the foundation for the university's strong basketball program; to the administration complex, which housed all financial operations of the university; to the needed performing arts center, which today serves as a vibrant part of university life. The building's original exterior is still recognizable and serves as a constant reminder of architecture's staying power at the heart of campus.

—DD & SR

Edward B. Bunn, SJ Intercultural Center (ICC) (1982)

Just north of the campus's historic core is the Edward B. Bunn, SJ Intercultural Center (ICC), an angular red brick structure of over 200,000 square feet. Dedicated to Bunn, who served as Georgetown's president from 1952 to 1964, the ICC's original mission was to join in the effort of bolstering US global education. The ICC continues to house the Georgetown School of Foreign Service (SFS) headquarters as well as numerous academic departments. The structure was designed by Metcalf & Associates, with Anshen & Allen of San Francisco serving as consulting architects; George Hyman built the ICC, which opened in 1982.

Described by one Georgetown student as a "red brick monstrosity," the geometric, streamlined design contrasts sharply with the gray-hued Collegiate Gothic style of Copley and White-Gravenor Halls to its south. In 1988 the *Washington Post* likened it to a "dark spaceship" landing on the historic campus.

The ICC embraces the north and west sides of the adjacent Red Square Courtyard, while its southern roof slopes sharply downward toward the Jesuit Community Cemetery. The building's angled profile takes advantage of the campus topography, maximizing its footprint space without overshadowing Copley Hall. Steep steps and a small outdoor theater platform sit on the building's southeast side. Perpendicular to the structure's southern

Edward B. Bunn, SJ Intercultural Center entrance.

Edward B. Bunn, SJ Intercultural Center.

section and bold eastern elevator tower, the edifice extends to the east over Carroll Walk. This walkway leads visitors to the north area of campus.

Consisting of seven stories, the ICC's central glass-covered atrium sits within the third, main level. This light-filled atrium includes open study space and a coffee shop. Housed within the ICC are the SFS Dean's Office and other university administrative offices, faculty offices, classrooms, a large auditorium, a language learning center, and computer facilities.

A nationwide assessment of opportunities for international education in the United States prompted the ICC's development. In addition, by the mid-1970s, the university's international programs and activities had outgrown its ability to house them. Following the Vietnam War, a presidential commission concluded educational resources in the international field were inadequate, and most agreed that improvements in American global education was pressing. In 1978 federal funds were set aside for facilities at Georgetown as well as Tuft's Fletcher School of Law and Diplomacy.

The ICC has been a pivotal campus structure, not only for providing dedicated space for leading global education but also for its pioneering role in the use of solar power. The 1973 oil crisis prompted interest in alternative

Rooftops of Davis Performing Arts Center, Edward B. Bunn, SJ Intercultural Center, Regents Hall, and Leavey Student Center.

sources of energy. In 1979 President Jimmy Carter had solar panels installed on the White House roof. By 1984 the ICC's roof had been renovated to incorporate over four thousand solar panels, at the time one of the largest rooftop solar arrays in the world. The installation served as an exemplary higher education project that sought to demonstrate how solar technologies could be used in place of regular building materials. The panels were integrated into the roof and were designed to be weathertight. They operated for roughly thirty years.

The installation, however, was not without flaws. The rough surface of the panels, a feature meant to decrease the glare of reflected sunlight so as not to affect planes taking off and landing at nearby Reagan National Airport, also made the panels difficult to clean and led to a decrease in their efficiency over time. Moreover, in 1985, after a cleaning effort caused some components to malfunction, the installation was shut down for ten months.

As a result of the ICC's mission in global education as well as its leadership role in renewable energy, the building was primarily funded by federal funds. The US Department of Health and Human Services and the US Department of Energy contributed a total of $18.2 million toward the building's construction costs, while Georgetown raised roughly $3 million for the project.

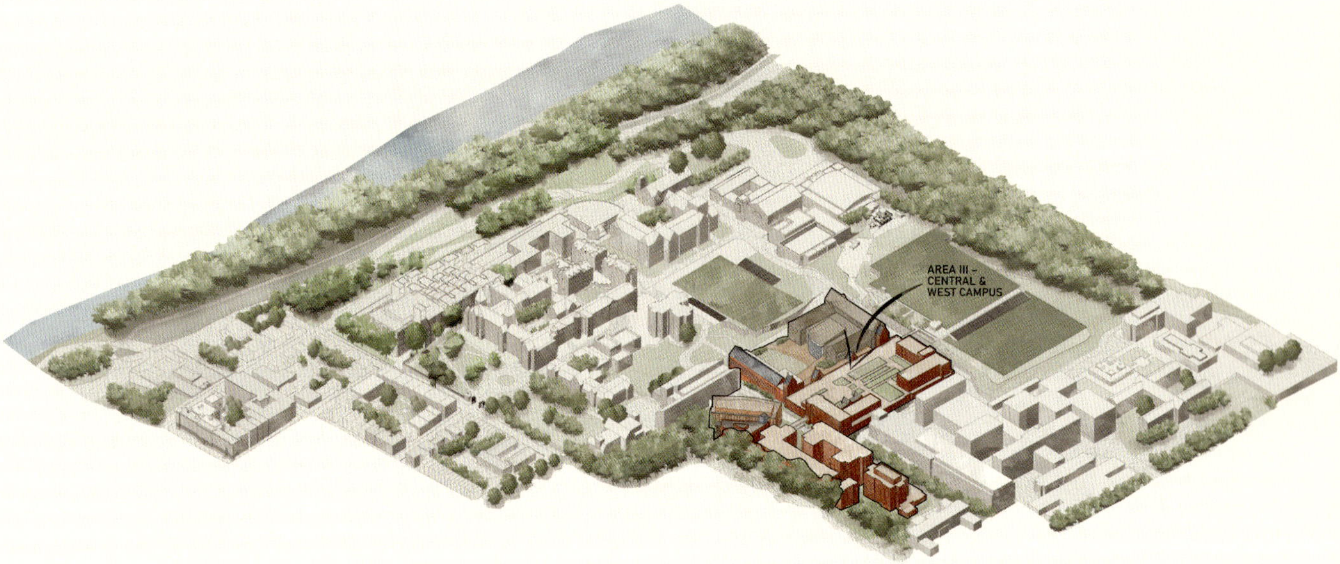
AREA III –
CENTRAL &
WEST CAMPUS

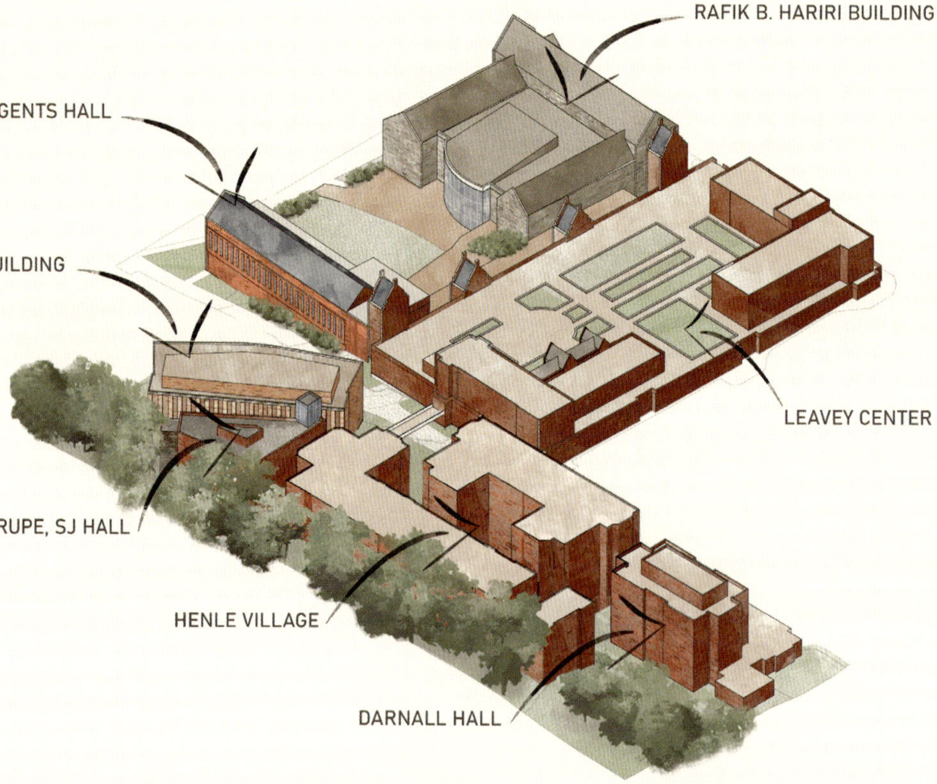
RAFIK B. HARIRI BUILDING
REGENTS HALL
REISS SCIENCE BUILDING
LEAVEY CENTER
PEDRO ARRUPE, SJ HALL
HENLE VILLAGE
DARNALL HALL

Area III

Central Campus and West Campus

The tightly packed central and west area of campus houses two key science structures, Reiss Science Building (1962) and Regents Hall (2012), as well as three dormitories: Darnall Hall (1965), Henle Village (1976/2025), and Pedro Arrupe, SJ Hall (2016). In addition, the late twentieth-century Leavey Student Center (1988) rests between Regents Hall and the McDonough School of Business's Rafik B. Hariri Building (2009). Below the business school, student athletes play on Cooper Field. This chapter begins with the Reiss Science Building, which rests along Carroll Walk across from the contemporary Pedro Arrupe, SJ Residence Hall. Beyond these two structures, a hub of campus activity lies to the west and north. The modern buildings in this area gesture to the campus's historical structures via their form and material, while broad swaths of International style transparent glass strike a modern chord within the Regents, Hariri, and Arrupe buildings and animate this campus hub.

The central and west structures arose to meet functional needs. In addition to the science centers, the Rafik B. Hariri Building brought the undergraduate and graduate programs of the McDonough School of Business into a single consolidated space. Boston-based architect Goody Clancy designed the Hariri Building using an open central atrium, which energizes the structure by letting in abundant natural light. Darnall Hall, which opened as a dormitory for women, and the coed Henle Village together served to ease the school's late twentieth-century campus housing shortage, while the Leavey Student Center continues to provide eateries, a bookstore, and other student services. In addition, the Leavey Center's former hotel now provides additional student housing space.

Reiss Science Building. Photograph by Peter Carter, 1980. (Georgetown University Archives)

Henle Village. Photograph by university photographer, 1978. (Georgetown University Archives)

Aerial view of campus prior to construction of Reiss Science Building and much of the development of Central and West Campus. Photograph by Ben Wells, ca. 1959. (Georgetown University Archives)

Reiss Science Building (1962)

The Reiss Science Building opened in 1962 during the Georgetown presidency of Edward Bunn, SJ (1952–64). The architectural firm of Thomas H. Locraft and Associates designed the structure; McShain Construction served as the builder. This streamlined, largely brick building commemorates Raymond Reiss, a Georgetown College alumnus and longtime school benefactor. Reiss graduated from Georgetown in 1919 with a major in physics, then went on to a career as a prominent national business leader owning multiple companies, including steamship, plastics, and rubber producers.

Reiss Science Building.

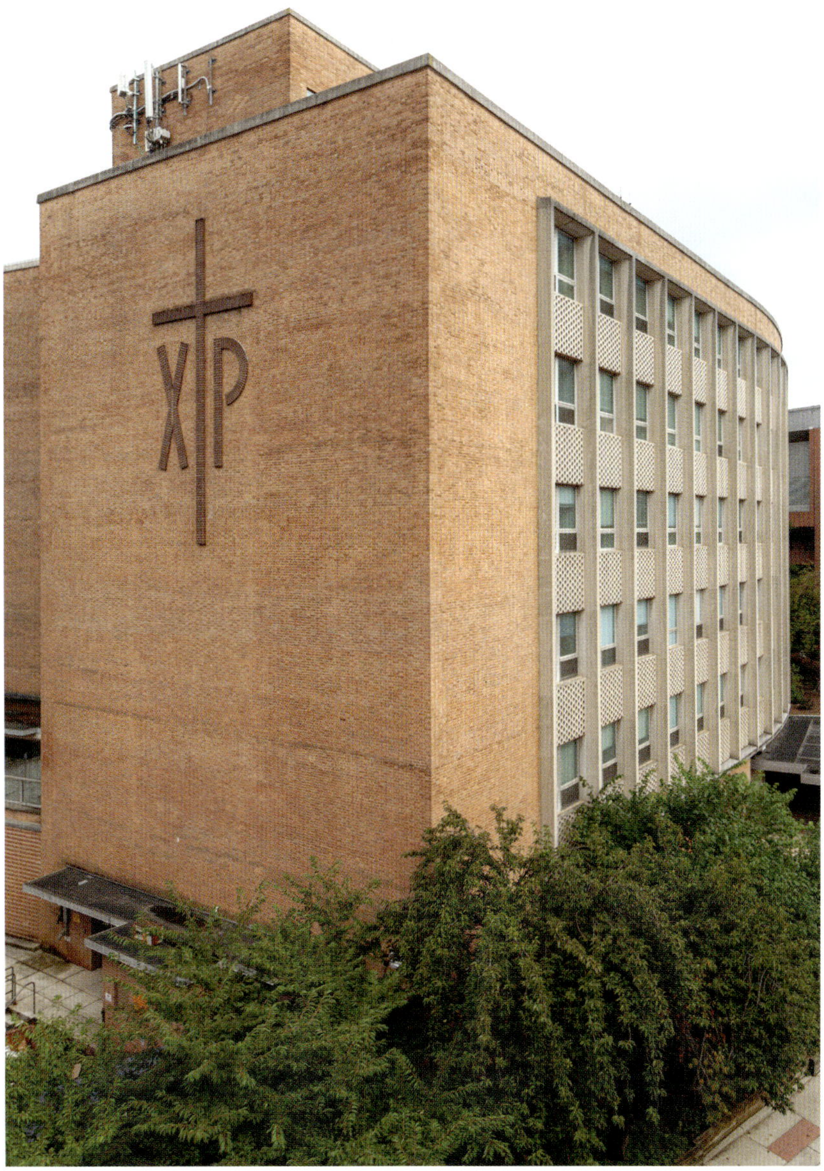

Reiss also had extensive real estate holdings in New York City, Chicago, and Detroit.

Formerly located beneath the Reiss Science Building was the College Ground, an area that served as a cemetery associated with Holy Trinity Church. Buried here during the early nineteenth century were free white people, free People of Color, and enslaved people. Holy Trinity Church records identify multiple individuals buried here as once belonging to the college. Although largely abandoned by the late nineteenth century, during the Reiss Building's construction some human remains were discovered and moved to the Mount Olivet Cemetery in Northeast Washington, DC.

Reiss Science Building now rests opposite Pedro Arrupe, SJ Hall to its east. On its eastern elevation, the Reiss Building's concrete cantilevered entrance overhang connects the structure with its mid-twentieth-century era. Reiss's generally streamlined form contrasts with the nearby Collegiate Gothic style structures Copley Hall and White-Gravenor Hall. The science building's more elaborate west facade curves outward and five-story piers, a myriad of boxy windows and hexagonal patterned screens, adorn the exterior. The Reiss Building's architectural style echoes work of the same era in Southwest Washington, DC, designed by pioneering female architect Chloethiel Woodard Smith. The building's west entrance foyer possesses a modern Art Deco vibe. Above the central wood and metal stairway, light streams through a geometric patterned ceiling, while a repeated design of silver tridents and squares neatly ornaments wooden doors within the foyer.

Reiss Science Building entrance foyer.

Locraft and his associates had previously worked on the east campus's Edmund A. Walsh Memorial Building (1958). Born in Washington, DC, Locraft received an architecture degree and PhD from Catholic University, then spent time at the École des Beaux-Arts in Paris. Early in his career Locraft apprenticed to well-known Washington architects Waddy Wood (1869–1944) and Jules Henri Sibour (1872–1938). Locraft also worked in partnership with architect Frederick Murphy (1879–1958) and led Catholic University's School of Architecture and Planning.

The Reiss Science Building emerged during the Cold War to meet the pressing national need for stronger science education, especially in industry and national defense. Although Perrot built White-Gravenor Hall to house the Chemistry Department, prior to the Reiss Science Building's erection the university's sciences remained scattered across multiple campus buildings as well as in the basement of Healy Hall and other temporary structures.

Providing key classroom and lab spaces, the consolidated Reiss Science Building cost roughly $4.25 million to build. The university received grants from both the National Institute of Health and the National Science Foundation totaling $600,000. An additional $2 million was raised in support of the design and construction of the building, with a large gift coming from Raymond Reiss. The building also houses the Bloomer Science Library on the third floor. Designed to seat 125 readers, this library provides research and other services to the university's science and math students and educators.

Pedro Arrupe, SJ Hall (2016)

The Pedro Arrupe, SJ Hall opened in 2016. The building rests on a narrow triangular slice of campus across from the Reiss Science Building en route north toward the university's Leavey Student Center. Arrupe Hall serves as a pioneering, modern model for on-campus residential life that includes transparent learning areas, social spaces, and a sustainable design.

The residence's name commemorates Pedro Arrupe, SJ (1907–91), a Spanish Jesuit priest who served as the twenty-eighth superior general of the Society of Jesus (1965–1983). Arrupe led the Jesuits following the Second Vatican Council, when the Catholic Church sought to modernize itself. Many consider Arrupe the Jesuits' "second founder" due to his leadership during broad reforms to the order in the 1960s and early 1970s. Arrupe pressed Jesuit priests to serve marginalized groups and fight for social justice. He emphasized the value of "men and women for others" and led efforts to help the Vietnamese people. While stationed outside Hiroshima during World War II, Arrupe survived the 1945 atomic bombing. Although Arrupe had left medical school to join the Society of Jesus, he used his skills to help the injured in the horrific aftermath of the bombing.

Pedro Arrupe, SJ Hall.

Visually, Arrupe Hall strikes a balance between geometric modern lines and continuity with the campus's historic forms. Composed of brick, glass, and colored stone, the building rises eight stories. The first story's blue, gray, and tan stones echo the colors found in the nearby exteriors of the White-Gravenor and Copley Halls. A stone tower rises from the structure's south side, which faces the campus's historic core. This tower's seventh floor includes an outdoor terrace with expansive views of the Washington Monument and beyond. The hall's brick central section, with rectangular fenestration, extends seven bays and is anchored to the north by a bold glass tower. Within this north tower are transparent glass lounges dedicated to student activities. Sasaki Associates Inc., a global architectural firm, led in the building's design, while Washington's StudioMB served as associate architect.

Developed for upper-class students, Arrupe Hall includes over two hundred beds. Each floor has roughly twelve rooms designed as suites for two, four, or six persons. Each floor contains a communal kitchen and social gathering room. Together with the seventh floor balcony terrace is a large study space. The open and flexible first floor areas operate as a learning hub; international living and learning communities reside in the building. Notable along the walkway lining Arrupe Hall is a social space with outdoor seating.

Representing the university's commitment to sustainable design, the Pedro Arrupe, SJ Hall received gold LEED status. The project's sustainable strategies include the preservation of mature trees on the site, an emphasis on natural light, a green roof, permeable paving materials that aid with stormwater management, and an enclosed bicycle storage area. Despite its gold certification and flexible multipurpose spaces, some of the building's doors failed to comply with weight limit regulations that are delineated in the Americans with Disabilities Act, and later required retrofitting.

Henle Village (1976/2025)

Architect John Carl Warnecke along with the Ehrenkrantz Group designed the 1976 residence, named in honor of Robert J. Henle, SJ, who served as Georgetown's forty-fifth president from 1969 to 1976. The builder was Glen Construction Company and the total cost of the project was $5.4 million. By the time Henle assumed office in 1969, there was growing pressure from the student body for the university to provide more on-campus housing. By the

Henle Village.

early 1970s the on-campus housing shortage was critical: In 1975 less than half of the university's undergraduates were housed on campus. With the completion of Henle Village in 1976, some 54 percent of students were living on campus. Only a small portion of the 1976 Henle Village remains nestled into the campus's north area, as the university demolished the majority of the late twentieth-century residence in 2023.

In the late 1970s Henle Village's thirteen red brick buildings of ninety apartments rested on a hill at the north end of campus. Sometimes referred to as "'Henleville,'" the townhomes were distantly modeled after Georgetown row houses. The apartment-style residence accommodated roughly five hundred students and encased multiple small courtyard spaces. On the west side, a series of maze-like ramps and broad terraced stairs formed an engaging entrance into the cavernous complex. Pierced by large rectangular windows of various sizes, the flat exterior walls of "the Village" looked like brick screens.

From a broad architectural history perspective, Henle Village distantly echoed the celebrated brick designs of Finnish architect Alvar Aalto (1898–1976). Aalto designed a dorm for the Massachusetts Institute of Technology in the post–World War II era, while Henle Village's terraced geometric form and community focus suggest Aalto designs found in Finland.

Reaction to Henle Village in the 1970s was positive, with one student even characterizing the brick residence as "plush." But Warnecke, who also designed Lauinger Library and Village A on the south side of campus, was careful to consider various "lessons learned" from Henle Village before embarking on the design of Village A. Among the elements taken from the original Henle Village that impacted Village A were an even greater need for common areas and outside spaces, the use of roofs as terraces, and an increase in student storage space.

Currently the university is replacing Henle Village with a much larger undergraduate residence by the same name. Also an apartment-style structure, the new residence hall is expected to house close to 750 students. It will be divided into two largely rectangular component buildings, Henle East and Henle West, with a green space in between. Along with the apartments, each building will contain lounges, a wellness space, and study rooms. Designed by Robert A. M. Stern Architects with input gathered from multiple campus stakeholders, it is hoped the new residence hall will secure LEED platinum certification. Compared to the late twentieth-century Henle Village structure, with its thoughtfully varied brickwork, asymmetric window placement, and engaging angled entry design, previewed plans for the new building appear rather hulking in scale and homogenous in form.

Darnall Hall (1965)

Opened in 1965, Darnall Hall commemorates Eleanor Darnall Carroll (1703–96), the mother of university founder John Carroll. Darnall is located along Tondorf Walk to the south of St. Mary's Hall. The blocky red brick structure with light concrete trim rises six stories above a ground-level base having a heavy cantilevered roofline. Large rectangular windows pierce the building's sides. Darnall's ground floor, now home to the popular Epicurean and Company, originally housed a student cafeteria that annually hosted a free Thanksgiving dinner for Washington, DC, seniors as well as other special events for notable guests, such as the city's mayor.

On the north side of campus and close to Reservoir Road, undergraduate residents criticize Darnall's distance from the main campus dining facility and library. Nonetheless, with double occupancy rooms on each floor centered around a common room, students highlight a sense of community fostered by Darnall's spatial layout.

When Darnall first opened, the campus newspaper referred to it as simply the "Women's Dormitory." Originally housing only female students, many of the building's amenities catered to women and included lounges, a music studio, and an area outfitted with sit-under-hood hair dryers.

Darnall Hall.

Darnall Hall. Photograph by university photographer, 1982. (Georgetown University Archives)

Darnall became a hub of social activity in the 1960s, hosting dances and other functions. Women were admitted to multiple university schools prior to Darnall's opening; however, it was not until 1969 when the college finally began accepting women that coeducational housing on campus began. By 1974 most of the dorms on campus housed both men and women, although usually segregated by corridor or floor.

—ET & SR

Regents Hall (2012)

Regents Hall opened in 2012 and sits across from the Rafik B. Hariri Building housing the McDonough School of Business. This modern science center forms the eastern side of an open quadrangle, with the Leavey Student Center to the north. A downward sloping green courtyard rests between the two buildings.

Designed by Payette Architects of Boston, Regents Hall contains 154,000 square feet of space that includes classrooms, teaching and research labs, conference rooms, and offices for the Biology, Chemistry, and Physics Departments. Designed to promote interdisciplinary collaboration, labs of

OPPOSITE: Regents Hall.

REGENTS HALL

the different sciences are placed in close proximity. Within Regents Hall there is also ample social space outfitted with vibrantly hued furniture.

Named for the university's board of regents, a key group of dedicated advisers, the dramatic structure is composed largely of glass and rust-hued panels. A flat roof covers the building on the west, while a sharp, thinly split gable anchors its southern end. Stairs lining the adjacent green courtyard guide pedestrian traffic into the central campus space. With five floors of open, streamlined research rooms and labs, the modern Regents Hall provides first-class space for science research and education, all of which was much-needed, as the nearby Reiss Science Building opened a full fifty years prior, in 1962.

Regents Hall also contributes significantly to the university's efforts to build environmentally conscious structures. The science center earned LEED gold certification. The heating and cooling system employs chilled beams, which is an energy efficient and environmentally friendly way to regulate building temperature. Considerable daylight from the large expanse of windows reduces electricity needs. Much of the building materials, secured from local distributors, are made from recycled materials, and designers chose furniture made of renewable materials for most of the building's furnishings. Payette Architects specializes in complex buildings for scientific research, higher education, health care, and corporate research.

Regents Hall cost nearly $100 million to construct, including a grant of $6.9 million from the National Institute of Standards and Technology, which helped to launch the Institute for Soft Matter Synthesis and Metrology. Housed in Regents Hall, this institute focuses on the study of various materials, such as gels and biological tissue. Received as part of the American Recovery and Reinvestment Act of 2009, the university received the grant in part because it employed hundreds during the building's construction and created permanent positions during a recession period.

Leavey Student Center (1988)

The Leavey Student Center, designed by Theodore Mariani & Associates, opened in 1988, although the desire to add a campus student center dates back to the 1960s. The building name commemorates Thomas Leavey, who graduated from Georgetown Law School in 1923, and his wife, Dorothy. The Leavey Foundation funding, as well as other monies, including a government grant, finally moved the project forward. Local architect Theodore Mariani's firm worked on numerous projects in Washington, DC, and on Georgetown's campus, such as the Washington Convention Center, the National Rehabilitation Hospital, the university's medical campus, Village C, and the renovation of Old North.

Leavey Student Center flanked by the Rafik B. Hariri Building (*left*) and Regents Hall (*right*).

Completed in red brick with light trim, the Leavey Student Center's arched windows and towers capped by stepped gables gesture to Healy Hall's inner western facade. A colossal structure, the Leavey Center encompasses over 250,000 square feet of space. The building forms a U shape at the north end of a central quadrangle that faces south toward the Potomac River. To the east a bridge leads visitors into the Leavey Center.

The student center houses a myriad of functions. A multilevel parking garage sits below much of the structure. A combination hotel–conference center–residence hall occupies the structure to the west, while the east-side section includes the bookstore and additional student services. In order to provide additional main campus undergraduate housing, the hotel currently functions as a student residence. Also within Leavey are religious gathering spaces dedicated to the Jewish faith as well as a Dharmic meditation center. The career office, a student-run store, restaurants, a faculty club meeting space, and a social/study space are among the complex's other elements.

By providing centrally located parking and hotel accommodations, the university aimed to consolidate activity on campus and reduce tensions that overflow into the university's surrounding community areas might bring about. The Leavey Center's green south-facing terraced courtyard associates it with the first stage of an academic village within the campus. In the 1980s,

Leavey Student Center clock tower and bridge.

university architect Dean Price considered this design a distant urban vision of Thomas Jefferson's plan for the University of Virginia. Although the Leavey Center anchors the cascading quadrangle, given its large-scale myriad functions and its bland interior spaces, the center can feel unwieldy. As the *Washington Post* observed when the building opened, Leavey addresses issues of scale and circulation with limited success.

Rafik B. Hariri Building (2009)

Located south of the Leavey Student Center, the McDonough School of Business's Rafik B. Hariri Building opened in 2009. While the lack of a centralized location had hindered the business school, the Hariri Building brought the school together within one commanding structure. Planning for the building began in 2003 and was part of a broader development project for the middle of campus, which included the construction of Regents Hall to the east and the renovation of Cooper Field to the south.

An $82.5 million structure, the capstone gift for the building came from Saad R. Hariri, past prime minister of Lebanon (2009–11 and 2016–20) and McDonough School of Business alum (C 1992). Hariri's gift was given in honor of his father, Rafik B. Hariri. Assassinated in Beirut in 2005, the elder Hariri, a successful business leader in the construction industry and an education-focused philanthropist, like his son also served as prime minister of Lebanon (1992–98 and 2000–2004).

Goody Clancy, a Boston-based architectural firm with strengths in sustainable architecture and preservation, designed the Hariri Building. Whiting-Turner Company served as contractor. The structure blends

Rafik B. Hariri Building.

Rafik B. Hariri Building.

modern and traditional styles. Echoing the historic structures on its north, south, and west sides, the Rafik B. Hariri Building's curved eastern facade employs glass and steel for a bold, transparent profile. In contrast to the modern east-side elevation, the rough-hewn gray stone and round arched entranceway on the south echoes elements of Healy Hall. Above, the building's sharp, steep gables reiterate roof lines found on the 1930s Copley Hall and White-Gravenor Hall. In harmony with much of the campus, the Hariri Building's red brick north and west elevations blend with the design of the Leavey Student Center. Making connections to the nation's capital, the Hariri Building's exterior sandstone panels possess a radial street design that echoes Washington, DC's map, dating back to L'Enfant's 1791 plan.

The five-story 179,000-square-foot business building's interior includes classrooms, study and meeting spaces, faculty and dean's offices, and a four-hundred-seat auditorium. A parking garage occupies the space below-ground. Natural light permeates much of the building's central glass atrium spanning multiple floors and providing city views at the uppermost levels. A dynamic, twisting central staircase with multiple landings and connecting walkways animates the building's interior. This staggered central walkway and impromptu meeting areas provide a main interior thoroughfare for business school students, faculty, and staff.

The building's component parts address the pragmatic needs of the McDonough School of Business. Hariri contains tiered classrooms, which foster class discussion. Study areas and breakout rooms address the business school's need for teamwork spaces. The auditorium hosts guest speakers and special events for both the business school and the broader campus community. LEED-certified, the Rafik B. Hariri Building employs water-efficient plumbing, recycled materials sourced from local companies, and an energy-saving lighting system.

The addition of the Rafik B. Hariri Building to the midcampus area set the stage for greater campus development and modernization. With linchpin business and science buildings flanking the terraced courtyard lawn, this central campus area serves key university needs and helped modernize Georgetown's architecture in the beginning of the twenty-first century.

—KR & SR

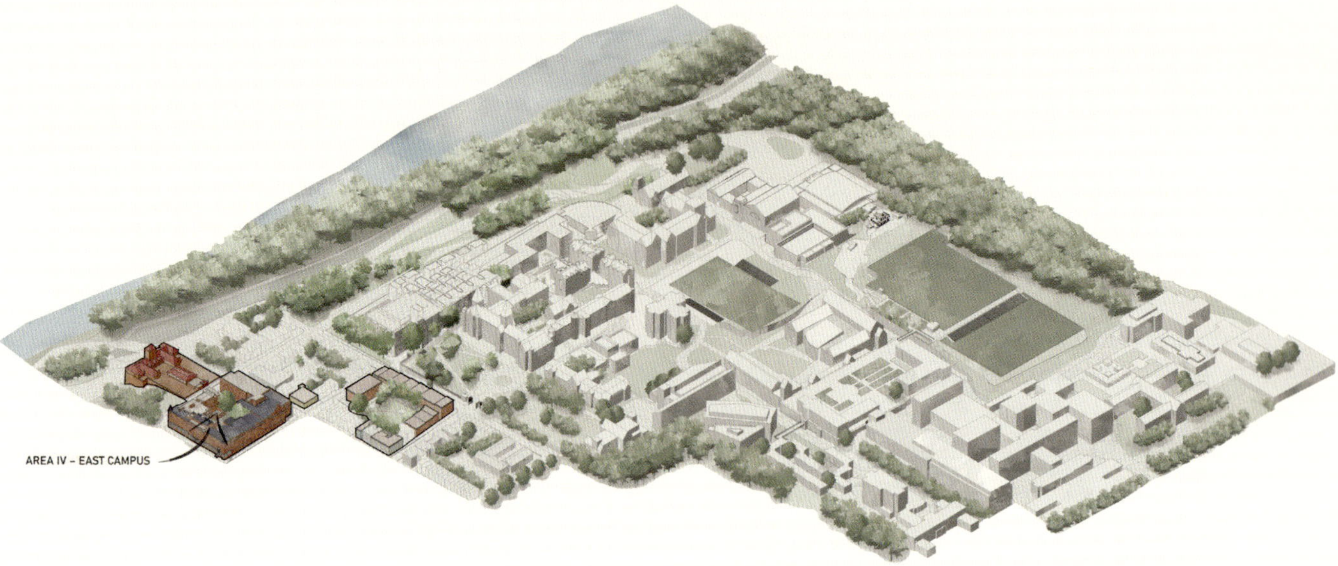
AREA IV – EAST CAMPUS

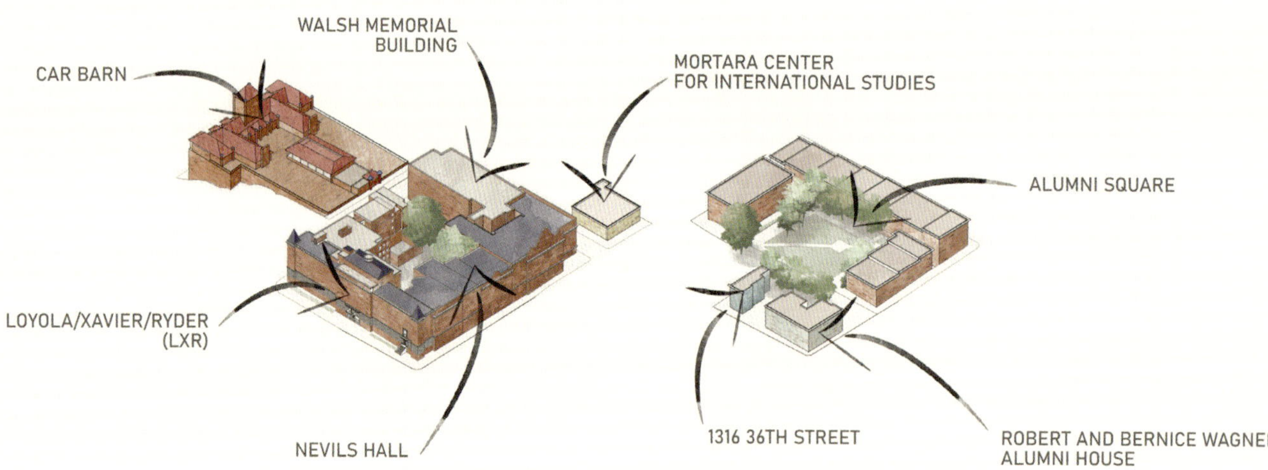
WALSH MEMORIAL BUILDING
CAR BARN
MORTARA CENTER FOR INTERNATIONAL STUDIES
ALUMNI SQUARE
LOYOLA/XAVIER/RYDER (LXR)
NEVILS HALL
1316 36TH STREET
ROBERT AND BERNICE WAGNER ALUMNI HOUSE

Area IV

East Campus

Embedded within the surrounding Washington, DC, neighborhood of Georgetown, the eastern section of campus sits outside the main campus perimeter. Georgetown was founded in 1751, forty years prior to Washington, DC, and Pierre L'Enfant's plan for the capital city left "George Town" just outside the new city's boundary. Georgetown finally merged with the capital in 1871. During the university's earliest years, Georgetown was a port city fueled by the tobacco trade; as historian Antoinette Lee highlights, from the waterfront, subsequent commercial development moved northward. Late eighteenth- and nineteenth-century merchants built prominent Federal style houses along Prospect and N Streets. As Georgetown evolved, additional residences, both stand-alone and row houses, filled the area. In the nineteenth century wood construction went out of favor, and the majority of Georgetown houses then employed brick. Among the nineteenth-century structures used by the university in this area are 1316 36th Street, the Mortara Center for International Studies at 3600 N Street, and the Robert and Bernice Wagner Alumni House at 3604 O Street.

By the 1820s, as the tobacco trade dwindled, Georgetown's central role and its overall economic prosperity declined, while Baltimore, a center for the flour trade, only grew stronger. Completion of the Chesapeake & Ohio Canal in 1850 bolstered the local Georgetown economy; however, it did not fully make up for tobacco's decline. By the early twentieth century the Georgetown waterfront had shifted to industrial use, including the appearance of power and meat-processing plants. In 1950, at the prompting of Georgetown's civic leaders, the US Congress officially designated the Georgetown residential area a historic district. Georgetown was the first historic district in Washington, DC, and the sixth in the entire country.

Within this eastern campus area and closest to the university's 37th and O Street entrance is Alumni Square residence hall (1983), while the Edmund A. Walsh Memorial Building (1958) resides further south along 36th Street.

President Dwight D. Eisenhower with Georgetown president Edward Bunn, SJ, at the dedication of the Walsh Memorial Building. Photograph by Georgetown University News Service, 1958. (Georgetown University Archives)

Robert and Bernice Wagner Alumni House courtyard.

The Maria & Alberto de la Cruz Art Gallery, as well as the Art and Art History Department, now reside in the Walsh Memorial Building. However, when it opened in the late 1950s, the Walsh Building housed the university's pioneering School of Foreign Service. Perpendicular to Walsh and lining N Street is Nevils Residence Hall, a student dormitory. Named after W. Coleman Nevils, SJ (president of Georgetown 1928–35), this dorm began as the university's first hospital building in 1898. In the mid-twentieth century the hospital moved to its current Reservoir Road location, and Nevils Hall, once converted for academic use, later transformed to its current residence hall function. Near to Walsh, the Loyola/Xavier/Ryder Building (LXR) is another student dormitory. Its largest component, Loyola Hall, was also part of the early hospital, opening in 1928. Two additional structures along Prospect Street merged with Loyola to become LXR in the 1990s.

Also noted within this section of campus is the historic Georgetown Car Barn. Designed by noted Washington, DC, architect Waddy B. Wood (1869–1944), this massive, late nineteenth-century structure lining M Street at the entrance of the Key Bridge served as a terminal for city streetcar lines. With its prominent tower and incorporation of wide round arches and brick material, the Car Barn distantly echoes Adler & Sullivan's pioneering Chicago Auditorium Building of 1889.

Walsh Memorial Building (corner view).

Car Barn, viewed from Prospect Street.

Alumni Square (1983)

Completed in 1983, Alumni Square is a townhouse-style apartment complex designed to blend into the Georgetown neighborhood. The work of noted local architect Hugh Newell Jacobsen (1929–2021), this residence for upper-class students sits diagonally across from the university's main entrance gates. Despite its ninety apartment units and close to four hundred beds, Alumni Square manages to echo Georgetown's small-scale row houses. The residence forms a U shape extending to the east along O and N Streets, with an interior green courtyard. Shade trees, benches, and a brick walkway ornament the courtyard enclave within the apartment complex.

Initially referred to as Village B, in 1986 the university renamed the four contiguous buildings Alumni Square in honor of a group of contributing

Alumni Square.

alumni: Wallace Groves (C 1923), Joseph E. Beh (C 1941), J. Nevins McBride (C 1929), and Eugene P. McCahill (C 1921). Along with their contributions, the government's College Housing Loan Program provided funding for Alumni Square as well as two other university residences: Village A (1979) and Village C (1987).

Beyond accolades for the university campus buildings, Alumni Square's architect is celebrated for his many home designs, which often combine historic inspiration with modern lines and abundant natural light. Jacobsen's clients included celebrities such as Jackie Kennedy Onassis; he also created an affordable house plan that was available for purchase via *Life* magazine in the late 1990s.

Jacobsen made good use of the building's sloped site: Its steep north-to-south drop-off encouraged the structure's stepped massing. He also utilized brick to express continuity with and respect for Georgetown's existing structures. Jacobsen described the Alumni Square facades as possessing a "restrained appearance, except for the deliberately over-scaled cornices and oriel windows that were abstracted from nearby predecessors."

The surrounding Georgetown community insisted on a cohesive architectural style early in the building process. In 1979 the Citizens Association of Georgetown (CAG) criticized the university's plan to build in what was then a vacant lot. The CAG considered the future student dormitory an "incursion" into the residential community and would lead to a disruption in its quiet atmosphere. In line with Jacobsen's approach, the CAG argued that, if the university was interested in maintaining Georgetown's historical integrity, the design should be "row house units much in the style of the surrounding homes."

Robert and Bernice Wagner Alumni House (ca. 1870)

The Robert and Bernice Wagner Alumni House is the home of the Georgetown University Alumni Association (GUAA). A complex of adjoining townhouses at the corner of O Street and 36th Streets NW, the complex of buildings is anchored by 3604 O Street and extends to three connected buildings on 36th Street. The structures, built around 1870, have been university property since the 1930s. The GUAA moved into the O Street address in 1951 and annexed the additional townhouses in succeeding years.

Officially formed in 1881 by a coalition of several alumni organizations, the GUAA has remained true to its original mission of maintaining the relationship between Georgetown and its graduates, fostering connections among alumni and encouraging participation in the university's interests and activities. The organization's early fundraising efforts contributed to erection of the 1912 statue of founder John Carroll that greets all who enter the main campus gates on O and 37th Streets.

Robert and Bernice Wagner Alumni House.

By the late 1990s the buildings that constitute Alumni House were in a serious state of disrepair. The GUAA office relocated to Wisconsin Avenue in 1998, and planning for major renovations began shortly after. Renamed the Robert and Bernice Wagner Alumni House after its major project sponsors (Robert was F 1948), the facility reopened in 2005, welcoming the association back to a significantly updated home. The improvements sought to preserve or match existing elements, such as the original masonry and windows, while bringing the building into compliance with ADA standards and modern building codes. A courtyard garden with a fountain unifies the shared outdoor space in addition to providing natural light and views for the interior offices. More recently, the university again renovated Alumni House.

—NA

1316 36th Street (ca. 1874)

This three-bay freestanding house is two stories tall with a projecting roof cornice supported by volutes. An arched entranceway marks its northern corner. Heavy molded lintels cap three rectangular shuttered windows on each story of the building. In recent years the building housed the Walsh School of Foreign Service's Institute for the Study of Diplomacy. However, the institute moved to 3610-3612 O Street, and 1316 36th Street now serves as additional student housing.

Visible in the many historic residences within this eastern area of campus, Georgetown homes generally display a conservative builder architecture tradition. In some instances, American and British pattern books provided sources of inspiration for early Georgetown builders. However, as historian Daniel Reiff highlights, the majority of Georgetown structures are

1316 36th Street NW.

vernacular in form, with minimal focus on achieving a particular architectural style. Many of Georgetown's homes arose when size and dimension were largely determined by lot size and the spanning capabilities of supporting elements. Wall surfaces are generally flat and details are additive. Among the many row houses that fill the eastern area of campus, little interest was paid to striking sculptural forms evident in the Tudor Place Estate designed by William Thornton (1815). A short distance from campus, Tudor Place is located in northeast Georgetown, a locus for some of the area's largest and most impressive homes.

A conservative Georgetown building tradition continued even after 1830, when the Greek Revival style was adopted for large-scale government buildings in the nation's capital. The democratic political associations embedded in the Greek Revival mode would not have resonated with the merchants and professional men of Georgetown to nearly the degree it enthralled Thomas Jefferson and prominent capital architects such as Benjamin Latrobe and Robert Mills. Nonetheless, the harmonious proportion and small scale of Georgetown's townhomes, as exemplified by 1316 36th Street, effectively transport the visitor to a distant past era.

Mortara Center for International Studies (ca. 1891)

The Mortara Center for International Studies, which opened in 2005, is currently housed at 3600 N Street NW.. A two-story brick structure that merges two row houses, the Mortara Center resides at the corner of 36th and N Streets. The building possesses an entablature and projecting cornice

Mortara Center for International Studies.

with corbeled brick detailing as well as long rectangular windows with arched heads. First-story bay windows front both streets. This building has served multiple functions over time, including operating as a Georgetown retail and clothing shop during the 1980s. Offices for faculty of the School of Foreign Service and the Center for Security Studies now reside here. The building's name commemorates Michael Mortara, a 1971 SFS graduate and past president and chief executive of Goldman Sachs Ventures. Mortara was a dedicated university volunteer and board member.

Nevils Hall (ca. 1898)

Nevils Hall, which lines N Street between 36th and 35th Streets, is named after W. Coleman Nevils, SJ, president of Georgetown University from 1928 to 1935. The imposing dark red brick structure now serves as a residence hall; however, Nevils Hall began as the Georgetown University Hospital, erected in 1898. Prior to the hospital's development, the site's N street land, with a frontage of 63 feet on 35th Street and 120 feet on N Street, had been in the possession of the university for many years.

Architects C. W. Keferstein and C. A. Didden designed the original hospital structure, and near the building's corner on 35th Street an inscription of "AD 1898" is marked on its attic story. During the hospital's first two decades, it expanded several times, as the number of patients treated there continued to rise. The Sisters of Saint Francis oversaw hospital operations during that time. In the first year alone, the institution treated over 450 patients. The varied roofline of the connected block of the N Street buildings testifies to the hospital's piecemeal growth.

The early hospital met a pressing Georgetown community need. In 1897 a reporter for the *College Journal* noted that old Georgetown had a large population but "lacked even the semblance of a hospital." Moreover, the *Journal* emphasized the hospital's ideal location close to the then-new Union Station (today known as the Car Barn), which was the terminal for four streetcar lines. The hospital cost roughly $30,000 to build and was funded primarily by private contributions from individuals such as the Washington banker Elisha Francis Riggs (1851–1910), who early on gave $1,000 to the hospital project.

After construction of the original building, an expansion was made adjacent to the east side and new wings were added on the west. Beside the earliest structure is the Lisner Memorial Building, dedicated in 1909. Two years later the university added a building dedicated to Riggs. On the same N Street block, George Kober (1850–1931), professor of medicine and dean of Georgetown Medical School, provided funds for a second wing. On the corner of 36th and N Streets another addition was opened to serve individuals with psychiatric illness. This corner building later housed nurses, and in

Nevils Hall.

View Along N Street before 1912. (Georgetown University Archives)

1924 the university dedicated it to Dr. Sofie Nordhoff Jung (1868–1943), the first woman member of the Georgetown University medical faculty, and her husband, Dr. Franz A. R. Jung.

Nevils Hall functioned as a hospital until 1947, when the university's new hospital opened at the northern Reservoir Road site. After the hospital functions left Nevils, the graduate school used the building, and it also has served as a dormitory for the college. In 1957 architects Murphy & Locraft renovated the structure, converting the building to a central spot for an array of important campus activities. Nevils was used for administrative and faculty offices by four different schools: the School of Foreign Service, Business Administration, College, and the Institute of Languages and Linguistics. Classes also were held in the building. Despite the changes in use and the passage of time, in 1976 a *Georgetown Voice* reporter observed that Nevils' had a haunting spirit, narrow winding passageways, and yellow hallways with buckled tile that "groaned" amid the old hospital walls.

In 1983 Nevils's function again shifted when the firm of Mariani & Associates was engaged to convert the building to a full-scale dormitory. Along with the opening of nearby Alumni Square, Nevils eased a major undergraduate housing crunch at the time. In its complete renovation of the historic building, the architects used a design that replaced infrastructure systems but kept the existing walls intact. The architects also added new windows and increased accessibility in the building. Echoing the past, the university divided the apartment complex into sections with the names of remembered alumni, including Lisner, Kober, and Riggs. The forty-six apartments accommodate over two hundred students and include features such as exposed brick, lofts, and balconies.

Loyola–Xavier–Ryder Hall (LXR) (ca. 1928)

Originally composed of three separate buildings—Loyola Hall, Xavier Hall, and Ryder Hall—in the mid-1990s the university renovated and connected the three to form one residential dormitory commonly referred to as LXR. The broader block of buildings formed by LXR plus the adjacent Nevils Residence Hall and the Walsh Building all share an enclosed outdoor courtyard.

Opened in 1928, Loyola Hall stretches along 35th Street between N and Prospect Streets and originally served as a wing of the university's hospital.

Loyola/Xavier/Ryder (LXR) Building.

Later, from 1947 to 1956, the School of Nursing occupied Loyola Hall. After 1956, however, it functioned as a dormitory and served other purposes, including space for counseling and psychiatric services.

Xavier Hall, close by on Prospect Street, originally opened in 1944 during World War II. Built with government financial support, Xavier Hall first served as a residence hall for nurses. Called Saint Mary's Hall until the mid-1950s, the university then transferred the Saint Mary's name to the new nurses' residence building on the north campus. Then named Xavier Hall, the structure served for a time as the International Student House. It is named for Saint Francis Xavier (1506–1552), who studied in Paris with Saint Ignatius of Loyola, SJ (1491–1556) in the early days of the Jesuit order.

Ryder Hall, also located on Prospect Street adjacent to Xavier to its west, commemorates James Ryder, SJ, president of Georgetown University (1840–45 and 1848–51). The planar brick building dates to 1898. Early on this building served as a residence hall for medical interns and hospital employees. The university renovated Ryder in 1948 and it later served as a dormitory.

Finally, in 1994 the university renovated Loyola, Xavier, and Ryder into LXR at a cost of $12.5 million. Reconfigured interior spaces increased the number of dormitory beds, and bridges connected the individual buildings to one another. LXR continues to serve as an important residence hall on the east campus. Among Loyola's notable past residents, US president Bill Clinton lived in the building during the 1964–65 school year.

Edmund A. Walsh Memorial Building (1958)

Designed by Murphy & Locraft Architects and built by the George A. Fuller Construction Company, Edmund A. Walsh Memorial Building opened in 1958 amid great fanfare. Though now regularly in need of repair, in 1958 a campus journalist described the new building as "magnificent, functional and modern." Completed during the presidency of Edward Bunn, SJ (1952–64), the Walsh Memorial Building was part of a phenomenal campus building campaign orchestrated by the mid-twentieth-century leader. Walsh lines 36th and Prospect Streets; before its construction a public school occupied the site. Rising four stories, including an attic level, the building has a streamlined profile. A dramatic, recessed multistory ivory entrance colonnade offsets its dark red brick exterior. A prominent university seal decorates the entrance doorway. Based closely on the Great Seal of the United States, the administration of Georgetown's third president, Louis William DuBourg, SJ (1796–98), adopted the first university seal. Within the emblem, an eagle carries both a globe (a symbol of rational knowledge) and a cross (the symbol of Christian faith).

The building commemorates Edmund A. Walsh (1885–1956), who founded the university's pioneering School of Foreign Service in 1919. Walsh had

Walsh Memorial Building.

an influential global career as an educator, diplomat, government adviser, and author. In its early years (1919–32), the Old Law School on E Street in downtown Washington, DC, housed SFS classes. Then the SFS moved to Healy Hall, where it stayed for many years prior to the opening of the Walsh Building. President Eisenhower visited campus to dedicate the building in 1958; the university awarded him an honorary doctorate of laws degree. In his speech, Eisenhower emphasized the global outlook underlining the

Architect's drawing of Walsh Memorial Building. *Deltasig of Delta Sigma Pi Newsletter*, May 1959. (Georgetown University Archives)

Hall of Nations in Walsh Memorial Building. Photograph by Bob Young Jr., 1958. (Georgetown University Archives)

mission of the SFS, noting, "We need people who see that no part, no matter how important, can be greater than the world." Eisenhower also praised SFS graduates as "soldiers of peace" who found satisfaction in serving their country and the cause of worldwide peace.

Along with classrooms and offices, a library, a conference room, language labs, a student lounge, and a public address system were among the amenities within the Walsh Building when it opened. The building's showcase, however, was the Hall of Nations, which could accommodate over four hundred. The hall displayed the seal of the United Nations and a myriad of country flags. Further marking the international mission of the building's occupants, French sculptor Pierre Bourdelle designed an enormous globe for the foyer. Made of plexiglass and lit from within, the globe was ten feet in diameter and made a full rotation every three minutes. The globe remained in Walsh until the building's renovation in the early 1980s.

The SFS was moved from Walsh when the Edward B. Bunn, SJ Intercultural Center opened in 1982. After renovations, the Black Box Theater took over the Hall of Nations space. Today the Walsh Building houses the Art and Art History Department. By 2018 the space once occupied by the Hall of Nations and the Black Box Theater was transformed again to function as the Maria & Alberto de la Cruz Art Gallery. The Walsh Building also houses the smaller Lucile M. and Richard F. X. Spagnuolo Art Gallery.

Car Barn (1895)

The Georgetown Car Barn is a separate building to the southeast of the main campus, bounded by Prospect and M Streets on the north-south axis, between 35th and 36th Streets. The university recently purchased the historic structure after leasing the space from the Douglas Development Corporation for many years. The Car Barn houses the Graduate School of Arts and Sciences and other departments.

In 1895 the Capital Traction Company engaged noted Washington architect Waddy Butler Wood to design a terminal hub for several streetcar lines. The Car Barn served as a passenger station and stored streetcars. It included an early cable car system; however, soon after opening, the Capital Traction Company converted its streetcars to electric power. The building later evolved into an office space, resulting in several renovations, most significantly in 1911, when an interior overhaul and facade renovation substantially altered Wood's original Romanesque Revival structure. Multiple arches and a prominently articulated tower distinguish the building's south side, which faces M Street. Today's smoother facade features two rows of rectilinear windows above street level. A curved pediment, which once crowned the opening at the base of the tower, now surmounts the third-floor windows

View of Car Barn from the south.

Car Barn. Capital Traction Company Union Station, 3600 M Street NW, Washington, DC. In *Historic American Buildings Survey*, ca. 1900. (Library of Congress)

in front of the tower, displaying letters that spell Capital Traction. The Car Barn's history reflects adaptive reuse in response to the changing needs of the Washington community. Although it began as a streetcar terminal, by 1950 it had been fully converted to offices for various tenants. From 1963 to 1975 the International Police Academy (part of the US Central Intelligence Agency) occupied a large part of the building. The Lutheran Brotherhood assumed ownership after foreclosure in 1992, followed by the Douglas Development Corporation's acquisition a few years later.

The National Register of Historic Places added the Car Barn in 2019. A significant rationale for receipt of this designation is arguably due to its architect, Waddy Wood, whose impressive Washington portfolio includes the US Department of the Interior Building and the Woodrow Wilson House. Wood also designed the East Capitol Street Car Barn for the Metropolitan Railroad, now converted into residential condominiums. But in popular culture the Georgetown Car Barn is perhaps best known for the steep staircase on its western side, which was built following extensive excavations to the sloped site and the construction of a retaining wall. The stairs have been a tourist site since being featured in the 1973 film *The Exorcist*, when they became known as "The Exorcist Steps."

—NA

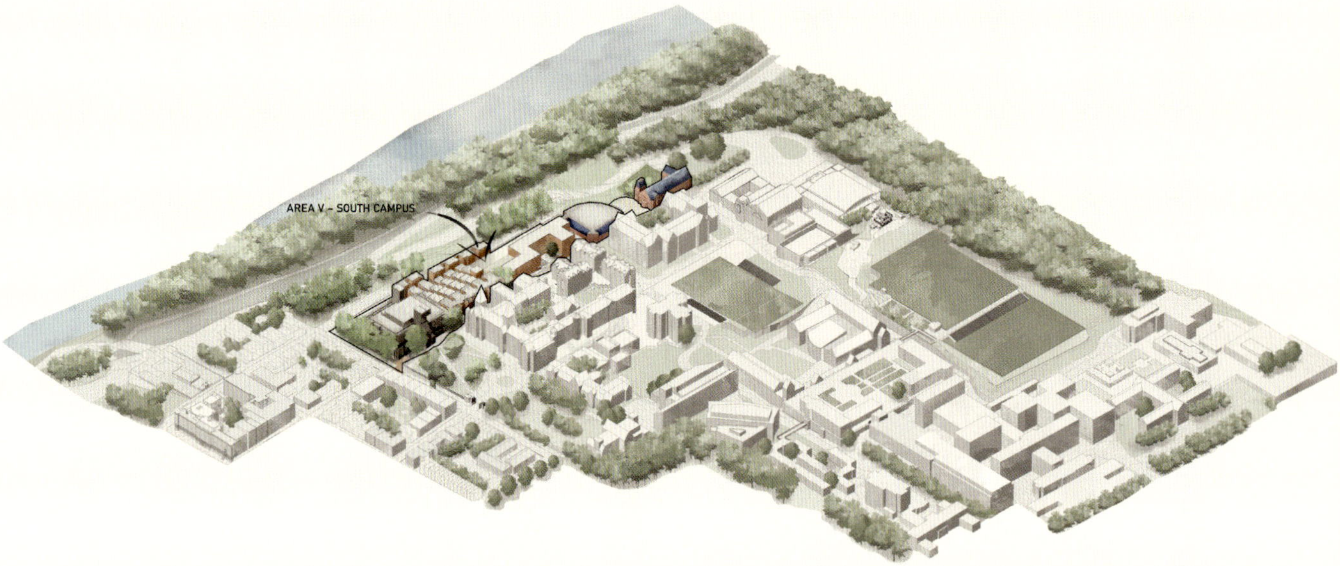
AREA V – SOUTH CAMPUS

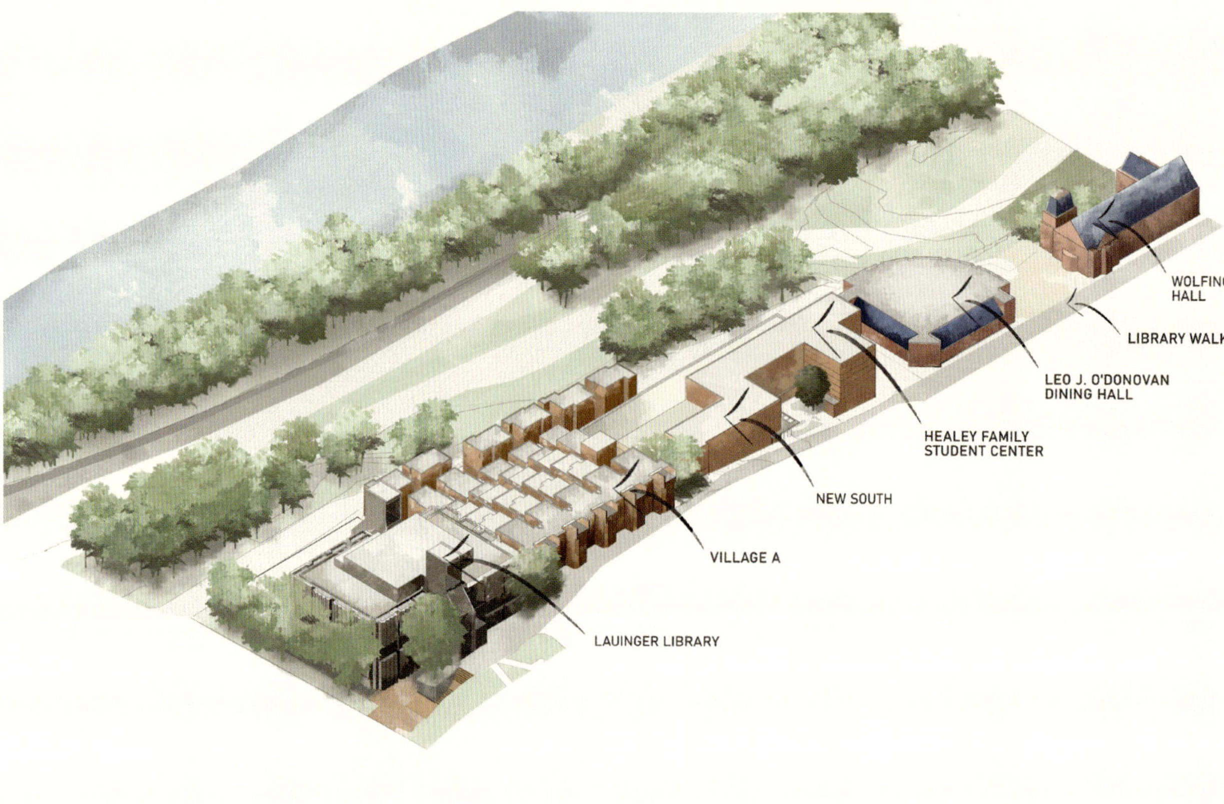
WOLFINGTON HALL
LIBRARY WALK
LEO J. O'DONOVAN DINING HALL
HEALEY FAMILY STUDENT CENTER
NEW SOUTH
VILLAGE A
LAUINGER LIBRARY

Area V

South Campus

The south section of campus extends east to west along Library Walk, with multiple buildings providing captivating views south to the Potomac River and Virginia. This area includes Lauinger Library to the east and ends with the early twenty-first-century Jesuit residence to the west. The university library moved out of the Riggs Library within Healy Hall to the Joseph Mark Lauinger Memorial Library in 1970. In the late twentieth century Village A was erected to provide additional on-campus housing in an apartment-style setting. John Carl Warnecke & Associates designed both Lauinger Library and Village A, and the abstract geometry of the residence's facade quietly echoes that of the library.

The oldest structure on this southern stretch of campus is the blocky, sprawling New South residence hall (1958). For more than four decades New South also housed a colossal campus cafeteria. In the early twenty-first century, however, the nearby Leo J. O'Donovan Dining Hall ("Leo's") replaced New South's cafeteria. Though the building continued to operate as a dormitory, in 2014 the architectural firm ikon.5 adapted the central cafeteria space to be a large living room–like student center, showcasing a great central fireplace, a host of flexible student spaces, and an outdoor terrace overlooking the Potomac River. With the two residence halls, the library, the dining hall, and Wolfington Hall, the Jesuits' residence, the southern quadrant is an integral element of the campus community's physical web.

New South. Photograph by Bob Young Jr., 1959. (Georgetown University Archives)

Old Cafeteria in New South. 1972. (Georgetown University Archives)

OPPOSITE: Lauinger Library south facade detail.

Healey Family Student Center interior. Photograph by Brad Feinknopf.

Joseph Mark Lauinger Memorial Library (1970)

Begun in 1967 and opened in April 1970, architect John Carl Warnecke's colossal concrete structure, the Joseph Mark Lauinger Memorial Library, anchors the southern end of the university's entrance quadrangle. The library memorializes Joseph Mark Lauinger, a 1967 graduate of the college killed in the Vietnam War. Joseph was the son of longtime Georgetown board of directors member P. C. Lauinger.

The sprawling library cost roughly $6 million to build, with nearly one-third of the costs covered by federal grant monies resulting from the Higher Education Facilities Act. A university capital campaign also aided in funding the library's construction. Prior to 1967, tennis courts occupied this site near the corner of 37th and Prospect Streets. Before the tennis courts existed, other athletic facilities, including a baseball field and an athletic track, occupied the space.

Rectangles and squares dominate the heavy modular library's five-story form. Small gray aggregate stone chips add texture to the building's concrete surface. Near the main entrance on ground level, an expansive reading room stretches to the west, with a central circulation desk and a study area to the east. Two floors exist below ground level, and there are bookstacks throughout the building. On the fifth floor visitors can take in a precisely framed glass view of the campus's entrance quadrangle, which appears like a large-scale animated painting. On the opposite, southern side of the fifth floor, the library's Murray Room, once a student smoking room, provides spectacular sweeping views of the city, the Potomac River, and Virginia.

Two blunted abstract-style towers project from the library's broad horizontal base. A taller front tower anchors the northern facade, with a smaller tower on the south side. To some extent the areas of the library can be "read" from the outside. The central staircase arises from within the front tower, and the entrance foyer and the ground level reading room are discernible from the outside. Study carrels exist in the vertical, saw-toothed projections visible from the building's exterior. The library's concrete towers, together with those of Healy Hall, strongly mark the view of the university and the city's skyline from Virginia.

The need for a new library dates back to the early twentieth century. Even as early as the 1930s, Riggs Library within Healy Hall needed more space for

Lauinger Library.

Students in what was the library's fifth floor smoking lounge, now Murray Room. Photograph by J. Alexander, 1970. (Georgetown University Archives)

its collection. By the 1950s the director of libraries, James Horigan, SJ, characterized Riggs as totally inadequate, and in 1965 Georgetown's president, Gerard J. Campbell, SJ (1964–69), noted that explosive knowledge growth, changes in modern teaching methods, and the growing number of faculty and students, especially graduate students, were all factors underlying the development of the new library. Moreover, there was a pressing need to improve the library to meet university accreditation standards.

Prior to Warnecke & Associates beginning the project in 1965, earlier 1950s library plans echo the sharp, blocky construction of the university's Hospital (1948) and Saint Mary's Hall (1956). With a projecting oriel window, the 1954 design also faintly incorporates the Collegiate Gothic style to blend with Copley and White-Gravenor Halls. Warnecke took a decidedly different tack, however, with the library's style.

Lauinger exemplifies the Brutalist mode that was in vogue during the 1970s. This style has multiple roots, but one key precedent resides in the post–World War II affinity for the large-scale concrete designs of Le

Corbusier. Brutalism's name itself is derived from *béton brut*, the French term for raw or rough concrete. Frank Lloyd Wright's fortress-like, no-longer-extant Larkin Building in Buffalo, New York (1904–6) or his concrete Unity Temple (1905–8) are early distant forerunners of the Brutalist style. In general, large-scale geometric concrete forms, expansive interior spaces, and varied concrete textures characterize Brutalist buildings.

Gaining approval from the city's planning and regulatory agencies for the library's design and site proved tedious for Warnecke and the university. The *Washington Post* reported that by 1966 the library had been the subject of four National Capital Planning Commission meetings, three meetings of the Fine Arts Commission, and two meetings of the Board of Zoning Adjustments. Despite Warnecke being a member of the board of the Fine Arts Commission, this group twice rejected the building's design and approved it only after Warnecke reduced the height of the top tier by 14 feet.

In addition to design concerns, the university considered multiple campus sites for the library, including those on which the Reiss Science Building and Village C now reside. By 1965 the university had narrowed the site choice to two—one across from the main gates on 37th Street and one on the current site within the entrance quadrangle. Changes to the District of Columbia's zoning laws ultimately removed from consideration the site opposite the main gates, leaving the library situated perpendicular to Healy Hall.

The library opened during the presidency of Robert Henle, SJ (1969–1976), during the contentious closing years of the Vietnam War. The building's

Sketch of proposed new library, 1954. (Georgetown University Archives)

opening ceremony was held at Gaston Hall, not at Lauinger itself, because Gaston provided greater security as it is embedded within Healy Hall. In 1970 security considerations were important, as university officials feared student demonstrations. Ultimately there were protesters at the dedication ceremony; protestors objected to the memorialization of a Vietnam War martyr in the building's name.

Along with the Brutalist aesthetic, Warnecke followed a contextual approach to the library's form. Visitors can, however, easily miss this aim of the architect. In 1965 Warnecke noted, "The most important exterior aspect of the library is its relationship to the older buildings on campus, especially the Healy building." The architect also highlighted what he perceived to be the "undulating exterior" of Healy as well as the nearby Copley and White-Gravenor Halls. Healy Hall's two vertical towers directly inspired the library's abstract spires, while Lauinger's gray color sought to echo Healy's hue. Most successful, however, is Warnecke's effort to design the library to balance the older structures that extend to the west of Healy on its south side. Lauinger's modular, repeated rectangular facade elements provide a well-balanced counterpoint to these buildings' blocky nineteenth- and early twentieth-century design. The library's projecting entrance provides an effective counterpoint to Ryan Hall. Unfortunately, multiple trees and plantings now obscure the clarity of Warnecke's geometry, all possibly in an effort to obscure the "ugly" Brutalist presentation.

Despite frequent contemporary barbs, in the late 1960s and early 1970s the architecture profession and the press lauded Warnecke's design. In 1976 the library received the Award of Merit that is bestowed by the American Institute of Architects in cooperation with the American Library Association. *Washington Post* architecture critic Wolf Von Eckardt noted that Lauinger's design was "a triumph of good taste compared with that hideous orange brick box, called the South Building [now New South], on the Potomac bluff, which is an insult to nature and architecture." In contrast to some campus critics, students gradually embraced the library's design. Eliza Lafferty (C 2021) observed,

> The banality of Lau's architecture—its heaviness, sterile lines, and gray color palette—initially appeared unwelcoming. Through the years, however, I have grown to appreciate the neutrality of Lau's environment. The simplicity of its design allows for people to populate and determine the space. Students may choose to focus on work in a cubicle, gaze outside through the tall windows, or walk around and socialize in the wide, open spaces. Dependent on the time of day, week, or season, Lau is changing—students define the spaces.

In an effort to bolster acceptance of the building, multiple renovation projects occurred in the early 1990s. The university removed the old card catalog and updated the third floor in 1993. More recently, several innovations have occurred. The opening of the Gelardin New Media Center expanded users' access to digital media, and the Booth Family Center for Special Collections now provides a state-of-the-art space for university archival materials as well as an improved area for teaching and exhibitions. In 2003 the student-run Midnight Mug café opened, and the expansive, albeit cavernous, second floor social/study space in front of the café continues to be a magnet for students. Still, Lauinger remains in need of revitalization. Plans exist for an addition to and modernization of Lauinger, with an emphasis on letting in more natural light, expanding open spaces, and providing greater vistas of and connection to the Potomac River.

Village A (1979)

John Carl Warnecke, described by the *New York Times* as the Kennedy administration's "court architect," designed Village A dormitory, Lauinger Library, and the north campus's Henle Village (which was mostly demolished in 2023). Village A's modern rectangular forms continue the aesthetic employed in the concrete Lauinger Library. Composed of red brick, Village A Residence Hall possesses interpenetrating exterior and interior spaces that enliven its site. Its four, three-story vertical facade projections create an ordered rhythm along Library Walk on the campus's south side.

Village A.

Village A staircase, looking north to Ryan Hall.

Between the towers, elongated rectangular windows pierce the otherwise heavy entrance walls and echo the geometry of the street projections. Designed with sensitivity to the sloping southern site as well as Lauinger Library's profile, four pedestrian walkways with plantings and benches extend through the building, fracturing the residence hall's mass. The walkways frame views of Virginia and the Potomac River from Library Walk. Toward the riverside, a central glass, steel, and brick communal room resides within a central patio.

The complex includes some 128 apartments with close to five hundred beds. Village A was the first dormitory apartment complex on campus designed to permit disabled access to over 50 percent of the units. This effort stemmed in part from a desire to comply with federal regulations passed in the 1970s, which aimed to prohibit discrimination based on a disability.

Lacking a particular donor, Village A's anonymous name remains. The Department of Housing and Urban Development (HUD) provided most of the $7.2 million building cost. Under this funding scenario, the university had to comply with HUD's requirement that the building contract be awarded to the lowest bidder—in this case Equitable Construction. Building began in 1978; however, a battle royale marked Village A's drawn out construction.

University administrators felt Equitable handled the entire project incompetently. Among the shortcomings were poor construction supervision, sloppy workmanship, and inadequate coordination among subcontractors. At the time, one construction worker surmised that not a single person on the building site had an overall concept of what was to be built. In the fall of 1979, as the situation sizzled, the *Georgetown Voice* reported "several hairy sessions" between Equitable and the university regarding construction problems. Due to the building's delayed opening, Georgetown had to temporarily house students off-campus in hotels and motels in Arlington, Virginia, as well as the Alban Towers in Washington, DC. Despite the delays and bad press, Village A began a phased opening in October 1979.

New South (1958)

New South, an expansive, boxy dormitory composed of heavy connected brick rectangles with a myriad of linearly placed windows, extends along Library Walk, with the Leo J. O'Donovan Dining Hall to the west and Village A to the east. Designed by Walton & Madden, New South opened in 1958. Federal funds helped support its construction and required the designers to follow an austere "no frills" architectural style. The dormitory

New South.

houses some four hundred first-year students. Its name pays tribute to Old South (1791), the campus's first structure, which was sited nearby on the opposite side of Library Walk (Ryan Hall replaced Old South in 1905). When New South's cafeteria opened in 1959, it was one of the largest nonmilitary food services in the Washington area and could accommodate over twelve hundred diners at a time. For many years this was the main place to eat on campus until the Leo J. O'Donovan Dining Hall opened in 2003.

Over the years, "ugly," "unattractive," and even "penitentiary-like" have been among the sharp barbs thrown at this mammoth south campus anchor building. At one point Dean Price, who served as university architect between 1970 and 1990, hoped to revise the barren style of the building. Historian Francis Ballman reports that the city's Fine Arts Commission rejected revisions to New South because the dorm was integral to the historic

Georgetown skyline. Despite criticism over its aesthetics, New South's strengths include its views of the Potomac and the ample size of its rooms compared to that of other residence halls. Further pluses of this large dormitory include its location near the dining hall and the infused vitality of the modern Healey Family Student Center, which opened within New South in 2014, taking over the old cafeteria space and beyond.

Healey Family Student Center (2014)

During the COVID-19 outbreak, almost all Georgetown students were forced to leave campus. There is no doubt that during the dark times of the pandemic, students felt nostalgic about the simpler things that they had typically taken for granted, such as hanging out with friends or learning with one another. That is why the Healey Family Student Center (HFSC) plays such a key role on campus, with its main purpose being the creation of a welcoming environment and the promotion of community across classes and schools. Ikon.5 architects designed the HFSC. Based in New York and Princeton, New Jersey, ikon.5 specializes in designing university buildings. Whiting-Turner Company served as the primary contractor for the HFSC,

Healey Family Student Center fireplace.

and the Philadelphia-based firm of Buell Kratzer Powell designed the HFSC's Bulldog Tavern.

The HFSC opened in 2014 and exemplifies adaptive reuse at its best. Inspired by the "Hoya Saxa" call, which is supposedly taken from the Greek and Latin words roughly translated as "What rocks," one of HFSC's pivotal design elements is its many gray stone walls. With over 44,000 square feet of space, the HFSC includes the showpiece Great Room, study rooms, meeting and social spaces, music practice rooms, and dance studios. The center encourages students to engage with the arts, as the dance studios have become increasingly popular in recent years. A ballroom and a student-operated café also reside within the HFSC.

Given the first-year students in the surrounding dorm, the HFSC fosters the integration of new students on campus. Among other events, the annual Council of Advisory Boards fair, which showcases Georgetown's clubs and activities, occurs at the HFSC. Moreover, the HFSC's location between "Leo's" Dining Hall and Lauinger Library makes it the perfect gathering spot between meals and studying. Students also often choose to work in the HFSC due to its meeting rooms with updated technology.

What the HFSC is best known for is its Great Room. This room effectively brings the outside in, with its expansive northern green wall and glass walls fronting the Riverside Terrace that overlooks the Potomac River. The Great Room is a communal space, an expansive yet cozy living room anchored by a large central fireplace. Student input was key to the HFSC's design, particularly with respect to Riverside Terrace, which was funded by $2.2 million from the Student Activities Fund.

The HFSC received LEED gold certification. Besides its green wall, other sustainable design elements include the use of skylights, lighting levels that depend on the natural light entering the space, and an exterior bronze solar screen.

—CP & SR

Leo J. O'Donovan Dining Hall (2003)

The Leo J. O'Donovan Dining Hall, named after Georgetown's forty-seventh president (1989–2001), is located in the Southwest Quadrangle, a complex of buildings that echo the spatial configuration and architectural materiality of the historic campus center to its east. The Southwest Quad is part of the expanded plan for the university that was designed by the pre-eminent firm of Robert A. M. Stern Architects.

Leo's, as it is popularly referred to, sits across from Wolfington Hall, the Jesuit residence just south of the quadrangle formed by the Kennedy, McCarthy, and Reynolds Residence Halls. The two-level, twelve-hundred-person capacity structure opened in 2003 as a state-of-the-art dining facility. It offers mobile

Leo J. O'Donovan Dining Hall.

serving stations for different cuisines, tables for four and eight, and floor-to-ceiling windows featuring expansive views of the Potomac River. The upper floor can host special functions, such as homecoming festivities and galas. A fifty-seat dining room on the lower floor includes audiovisual projection devices and group event amenities.

In 2015, in response to student feedback citing a need for more flexible seating arrangements, the university replaced the hall's round eight-person tables with smaller square tables. The smaller-scale tables also allowed for the accommodation of more chairs in the hall. Two years later, additional updates included a new central staircase with stadium seating on each side.

—NA

Wolfington Hall (2003)

Wolfington Hall, the residence for the university's Jesuit community, is situated on the river side of the Southwest Quad complex, which opened in 2003 along with the Leo J. O'Donovan Dining Hall and Kennedy, McCarthy, and Reynolds Residence Halls. Wolfington is the first building on campus

Wolfington Hall.

to be built specifically for the university's Jesuit community. For the nearly 150 years before moving into Wolfington, Jesuits often resided within buildings on the south side of the main Quadrangle—in Isaac Hawkins Hall, Ryan Hall, or Gervase Hall (structures now frequently referred to as the Former Jesuit Residence).

Designed by Kleinrock Studio Architecture to address the intellectual, spiritual, and recreational dimensions of Jesuit life, the four-story building houses a chapel, meeting spaces, a library, a dining room, and three floors of private residences with assisted living capabilities. An outside patio overlooks the Potomac River and the Canal Road entrance to the university. The brick facade harmonizes with the surrounding campus architecture, while its moderately asymmetric profile references Healy Hall's picturesque roofline.

The building is named in honor of Vince Wolfington (CAS 1962), varsity basketball player, successful businessman, and a longtime supporter of the Jesuit community at Georgetown. A former member of the university's board of directors and a cofounder of the George F. Baker Scholars Program, Wolfington received the John Carroll Award, the highest alumni honor, in 2003.

—NA

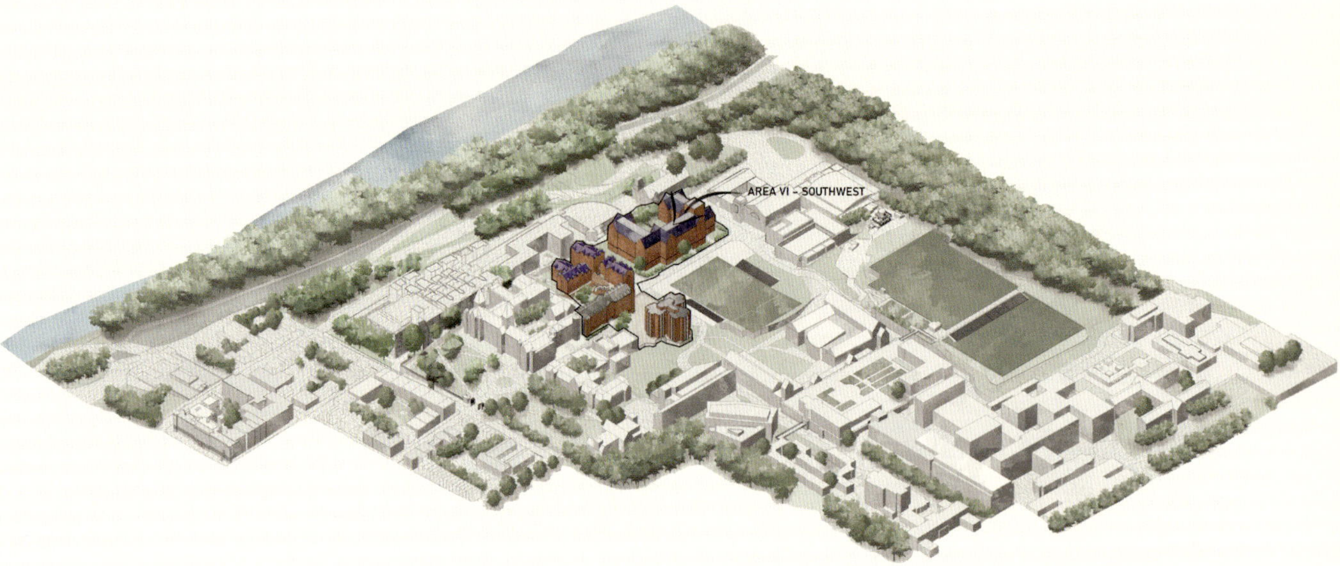
AREA VI - SOUTHWEST

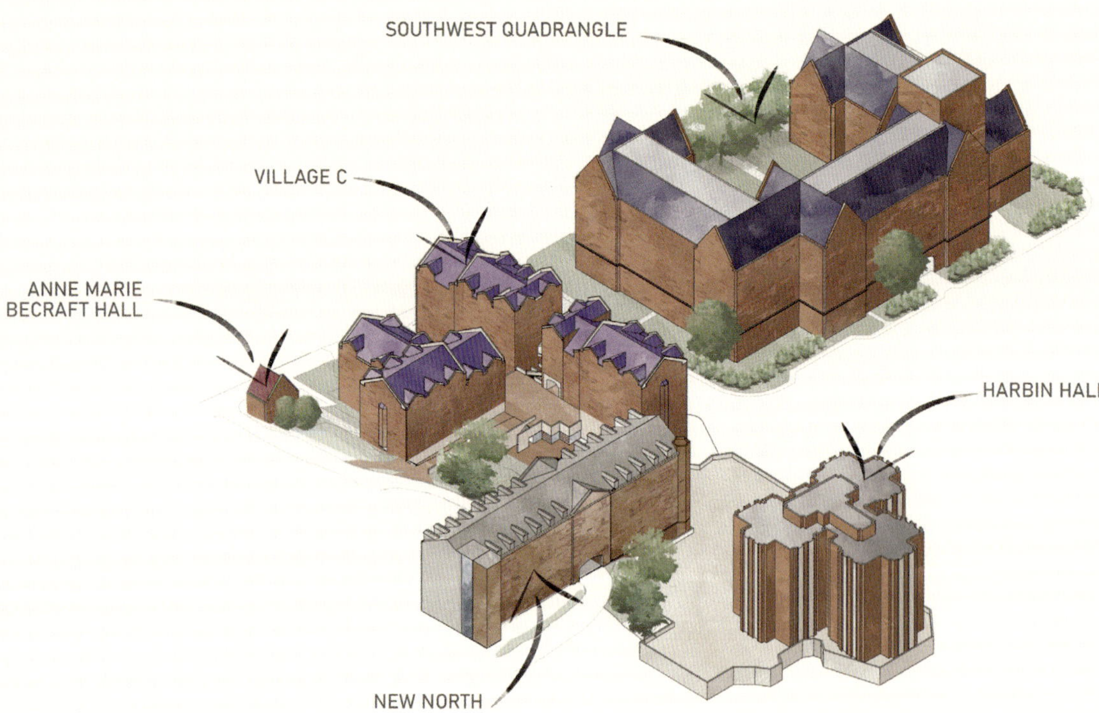
SOUTHWEST QUADRANGLE
VILLAGE C
ANNE MARIE
BECRAFT HALL
HARBIN HALL
NEW NORTH

Area VI

Southwest Campus

The southwest section of campus incorporates one of the university's oldest structures, Anne Marie Becraft Hall (ca. 1792), as well as extensive early twenty-first-century student residences designed by Robert A. M. Stern Architects, namely, Kennedy, McCarthy, and Reynolds Halls further to the west. Also within this area is the Mariani-designed Village C dormitory. Stern's connected dorms, together with Village C, which opened in the late twentieth century, provide housing for over fifteen hundred students and, with their opening, greatly increased the percentage of students living on campus.

The historic Becraft Hall commemorates Anne Marie Becraft (1805–33), a pioneering African American woman educator and nun who founded a school in Georgetown. Becraft Hall resides on the slope of Library Walk and currently serves as home of the John Main Center for Meditation and Interreligious Dialogue. Beyond Becraft and serving as an addition to Old North is New North, which opened in 1926 as a dormitory and classroom building. New North, which houses the McNeir Auditorium, resides above and on either side of Old North Way. Guastavino vaults cover the passageway along this campus walkway. Further to the north is the first high-rise dormitory, Harbin Hall. Originally designated for men only, Harbin Hall opened in 1965. By student accounts, Harbin Hall's unique clover-shaped plan helps foster a sense of campus community.

Groundbreaking ceremony for New North. Photograph by Underwood & Underwood, 1925. (Georgetown University Archives)

Harbin Hall, ca. 1965 facade detail. Photograph by Campbell Photo Services. (Georgetown University Archives)

Anne Marie Becraft Hall (ca. 1792)

Anne Marie Becraft (1805–33) was a free Black woman who pioneered education for African Americans in Washington, DC, and was one of the country's first Black nuns. When she was fifteen years old, she founded a school for young Black girls on Dumbarton Street in Georgetown. In 1831 Becraft joined the Oblate Sisters of Providence, one of the nation's earliest African American Catholic religious orders and assumed the name Sister Mary Aloysius. On April 18, 2017, Georgetown University renamed this brick structure, situated along Library Walk and formerly known as McSherry Hall, in her honor.

William McSherry, SJ, president of Georgetown from 1838 to 1839, oversaw the sale of 272 enslaved individuals living in Jesuit-owned plantations in Maryland to two Louisiana planters in 1838. He and his predecessor, Thomas Mulledy, SJ, supported the transaction to help pay for the college's debts,

Anne Marie Becraft Hall.

in part resulting from campus building expansion. In 2015 student protests prompted university president John DeGioia to establish the Working Group on Slavery, Memory, and Reconciliation, which recommended the renaming of McSherry Hall. It was temporarily known as Remembrance Hall, and later an official ceremony bestowed its present designation.

Tradition holds that Becraft Hall dates to 1792 and was initially used for horse stables as well as a storage area for construction tools. A college bakery operated out of the building in the 1860s; it housed the university archives in the 1890s. In the twentieth century it served a variety of functions: as a pressing shop, as workspace for the Biology Department, as offices for the *Georgetown Voice* student newspaper, as the site for Grounds and Landscaping, and later for the Office of Telecommunications. Since 2005 it has been the home of the John Main Center for Meditation and Interreligious Dialogue.

—NA

New North (1926)

Designed by the local firm of Marsh and Peter, New North opened in 1926 during the university presidency of Charles Lyons, SJ (1924–28). New North extends west from Old North, continuing the northern arm of this historic campus quadrangle. Marsh and Peter employed a spare Colonial Revival style for the new building, which aligns New North with Old North. The

New North.

builders laid New North's exterior brick in a Flemish bond pattern, which echoes that of multiple surrounding quadrangle structures. In Flemish bond each brick's long side (the stretcher) joins another brick's short side (the header). In alternating layers, builders place headers above the stretchers. Marsh and Peter used contrasting Indiana limestone for the building's keystones, windowsills, and doorways, and relied on fireproof materials, including reinforced concrete, for the building's interior. When New North first opened it included more than 120 dorm rooms, four lecture rooms, and an auditorium named after George McNeir (LLB 1881), a previous university regent. In addition, the basement contained a central heating unit and an ROTC rifle range.

Architecturally notable here is the passageway that runs through New North. The Guastavino Tile Company designed the arch covering this walkway. Spanish architect Rafael Guastavino (1842–1908) pioneered and patented this vaulting system, which is employed in many prominent American buildings designed by leading architects in the late nineteenth and early twentieth centuries. Among the many structures incorporating Guastavino's work is McKim, Mead & White's Boston Public Library (1895). This unique vaulting system uses thin interlocking tiles, sometimes

New North brick detail.

placed in a herringbone pattern, combined with layers of mortar to form a flexible and durable vault. An advantage of Guastavino vaulting is that it does not require centering during construction.

A noted local firm, included among Marsh and Peter's other early twentieth-century work in Washington, DC, is the Georgetown Riggs Bank (now PNC) Building at the corner of Wisconsin Avenue and M Street, NW (1921–22); the *Evening Star* newspaper building (1908); and William Syphax Public School (1901), a historically Black elementary school named after the first African American president of the Board of Trustees of Colored Schools of Washington and Georgetown.

Harbin Hall (1965)

Harbin Hall is one of the most easily distinguishable buildings on campus with its novel sharp geometric shape and towering nine-story stature. As the first high-rise on campus, Harbin stands in stark contrast to the university's historic core as well as its neighbors, such as the Davis Performing Arts Center, New North, and the Intercultural Center. Nonetheless, Harbin's brick facade remains in sync with much of the campus. The building is practical by design: The architects designed Harbin Hall to accommodate a large number of students on a limited piece of land, and to this day it does just that. Moreover, this modern building, with its distinct, angular clover-shaped plan, promotes a supportive residence community on each floor.

Harbin Hall.

The official opening ceremony of Harbin Hall was held on November 16, 1965, with much fanfare and ample blessings. The building had already begun housing students more than a year earlier, in September 1964. Interestingly, even as students started living on the first four floors of the building, the residence hall did not yet have a formal name. In December 1964 the school newspaper, *The Courier*, characterized the new building as a "huge, expensive pile of bricks known by the highly original title of 'New Men's Dorm.'" Before ultimately deciding the dorm would commemorate George J. Harbin, a professor of mathematics at the university for more than twenty-five years, there was discussion of naming the residence after President John F. Kennedy.

During the 1960s, Harbin Hall, along with Darnall Hall, helped meet the university's severe on-campus housing shortage. At the time, many undergraduates were living off campus and existing dorms were aging. The university developed Darnall Hall, located close to Reservoir Road to the north, in conjunction with Harbin Hall as exclusively women's and men's dormitories, respectively. Together with two other smaller projects, the university took out a loan of over $4 million to cover the cost of constructing the two halls, with over half of the budget set aside for Harbin Hall. Harbin would house over four hundred male students. The architectural firms responsible for the project were Cooper & Auerbach and Walton & Madden, two local architectural firms. Together the two firms designed this high-rise, stocked with three student lounges on the first floor, each equipped with private music rooms, Ping Pong tables, and televisions.

Rejecting historical modes for a more modern, efficient style, Harbin Hall's architects took note of contemporary trends. Influences of the pioneering architect Le Corbusier are apparent in Harbin Hall's elevated base pilotis, while the streamlined verticality of Mies van der Rohe's high-rise apartment and corporate structures are also distantly echoed here.

The erection of a modern high-rise on a university campus was not unique to Georgetown; as architectural historian Carla Yanni notes, after World War II, "skyscraper residence halls burst into the clouds at many universities." With a torrent of new students attending, colleges had to accommodate more students, and quickly. Residence halls were erected across the country using as little precious space as possible. In 1967 Ohio State University built two massive octagonal towers, the Morrill and Lincoln Towers, designed by Schooley, Cornelius, & Schooley. Although designed on a larger scale, the vertically impressive Ohio high-rise residences are similar to Harbin Hall: All possess a geometric profile and continue to be some of the tallest buildings on their respective campuses.

Not only is Harbin Hall's modern design unique on Georgetown's campus, but so is its layout. Arguably Harbin's most important feature is seen within its walls. Harbin Hall rejects the cookie-cutter long corridor plan in favor of a more communal layout. Eight double rooms placed around a common bathroom, repeated three times on a floor, gives Harbin its signature three-leaf clover shape. With only sixty students per floor and centrally located lounges and elevators, community-building is encouraged and easy to create. This design facilitates first-year student interaction and fosters close friendships and bonds early on in the college experience. Three "leafs" per floor allow for a mixture of male and female students on every level, except for the ninth floor, the "Ninery," an all-women's floor.

On a personal note, Harbin Hall has a special place in my heart. As a bright-eyed freshman moving across the country to attend Georgetown, living on Harbin Eight made the transition surprisingly smooth and effortless. I was lucky to meet all my closest friends on my floor thanks to the community-driven cluster system. My best friends to this day are from Harbin Eight and those first few weeks of classes. The rooms are spacious, especially when the beds are bunked, and the window seats in each room allow for comfortable lounging and scenic views of campus. I wish I could have experienced the original first-floor lounges, for now they have been converted to administrative offices. Regardless, Harbin Hall is an essential part of campus and has single-handedly shaped my Georgetown experience for the better.

—ML

Village C (1987)

Designed by Mariani & Associates, the Village C residence hall sits to the west of the campus's historic core of structures. In addition to designing Village C, Mariani's work on campus includes medical buildings, the Thomas and Dorothy Leavey Student Center, and an update to Old North in the early 1980s. A colossal, three-building complex, Village C hugs the hill as it slopes downward. Composed of red brick with light stone trim, the hall's roofline has stepped elevations. Bay, lunette, and circular windows contribute to the decor of this sprawling student residence. Village

Village C.

C's materiality and Modernist Revivalism exemplifies the Postmodern style prevalent in American architecture in the late twentieth century. The dorm's complex form, consisting of over-scaled window lintels, exterior blue-and-red accent hues, and abstracted Palladian-style window motifs, together highlight the playfulness and tendency to manipulate historical forms typical of the Postmodern style.

This residence hall provides housing for some seven hundred students. With its opening in 1987, nearly three-quarters of the university's undergraduates were then living on campus. Along with serving as a student dorm, Village C has also housed the university's Department of Public Safety, Health Education Services, and Department of Outdoor Education. Highlighting the multiple faiths practiced on campus, Village C houses a small Muslim mosque as well.

Divided between east and west buildings, Village C West possesses sixteen floors, while Village C East has ten. Common rooms exist on each floor for socializing and studying. Village C's double occupancy rooms have private bathrooms, prompting a *Georgetown Voice* reporter to observe that residents are "spared from witnessing the beauty and horror of what might happen in a college communal bathroom."

Prior to Village C's development, O'Gara Hall resided on the site. Built in 1874, O'Gara Hall was a wooden barn later repurposed as a carpenter shop and storehouse in the early 1920s. In 1946, after renovation, O'Gara

O'Gara Hall on the site that Village C now occupies. Photograph by W. F. Walsh, 1946. (Georgetown University Archives)

functioned as a dorm to meet the heightened need for student housing in the post–World War II era. Later O'Gara served as the school infirmary and housed the offices of the *Georgetown Voice*. In 1984 the university demolished O'Gara Hall to make room for the erection of Village C.

O'Gara Hall commemorates Martin O'Gara, SJ, who died in a plane crash while returning to the United States after World War II. O'Gara, a member of Georgetown's religion faculty, left the university in 1943 to serve as an Army Air Force chaplain. O'Gara's plane was flying from India when it caught fire. O'Gara gave his parachute to a fellow serviceman and helped other passengers escape.

Southwest Quadrangle (2003)

The Southwest Quadrangle residence halls, designed by the celebrated firm of Robert A. M. Stern Architects, boosted the university's on-campus housing capacity significantly. The university had not expanded its campus housing structures since Village C opened in 1987. Before the Southwest Quad's development, this area of campus functioned as a parking lot, extending from Village C to the McDonough Gymnasium. Opening in 2003, the mammoth brick-and-limestone residences include Kennedy, McCarthy, and Reynolds Halls. The Stern-designed dorms together provide housing for some nine hundred students, and when they opened they increased the number of undergraduates living on campus from roughly 78 to 90 percent.

A preeminent leader in American architecture, Robert Stern served as dean of the Yale University School of Architecture from 1998 to 2016. Based in New York City, Stern's private firm completes projects across the globe. Among the company's commissions are buildings for Yale University, Harvard University, the University of Virginia, Pomona College, and many other US colleges and universities. Sensitive to their context, Stern's modern buildings frequently possess a classical or historical component. Along with the Stern design firm, Clark Construction oversaw the building of the residence halls.

The southwest complex has three buildings set in a U-shaped configuration, with a central courtyard open toward the Potomac River to the south. In their material and orientation, the larger buildings echo Georgetown's earlier brick-and-stone buildings to the east. The three dorms share a connected ground floor, which includes numerous facilities such as reading and seminar rooms, recreational areas, and computer space. Students live in the upper floors, with McCarthy and Kennedy Halls rising eight stories, while Reynolds Hall has six floors.

Named after long-term Georgetown supporters, Kennedy Hall commemorates John R. (C 1952) and Elizabeth Kennedy. John Kennedy served on multiple university boards and participated in fundraising campaigns.

McCarthy Hall recognizes Thomas McCarthy, the son-in-law of Thomas and Dorothy Leavey, contributors to the Leavey Student Center. McCarthy led university fundraising efforts and served in several advisory roles. Also honored is the Reynolds family, who supported the university as alumni, donors, and board members beginning with Thomas A. Reynolds Sr. (L 1924). Within Reynolds Hall, the McShain Community Room provides programming space for campus events. This room honors John McShain, a member of the university's board of directors, who was a leading general contractor in the Washington, DC, area. Beyond the campus, McShain worked on construction of the Pentagon, the Jefferson Memorial, and the Kennedy Center as well as renovations to the White House. Along with memorializing key community figures, it is notable that the residence halls have housed numerous living and learning programs, including one focused on culture and performance and another on health and wellness.

Kennedy Hall in the Southwest Quadrangle, designed by Robert A.M. Stern Architects. Photograph by Peter Aaron/OTTO

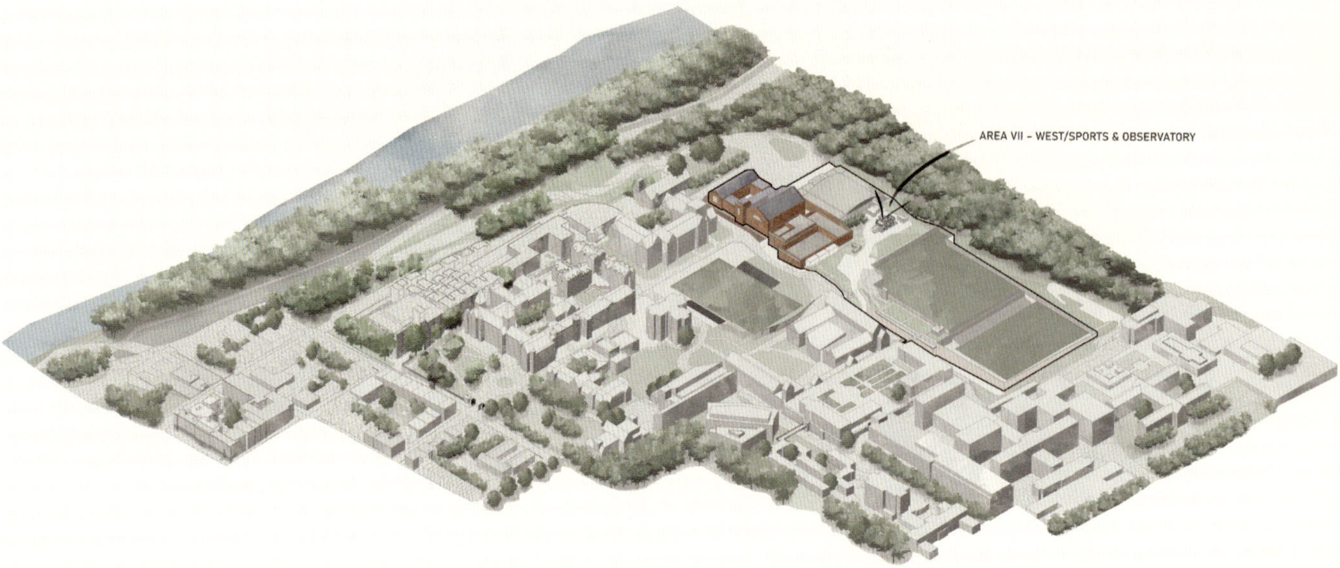
AREA VII – WEST/SPORTS & OBSERVATORY

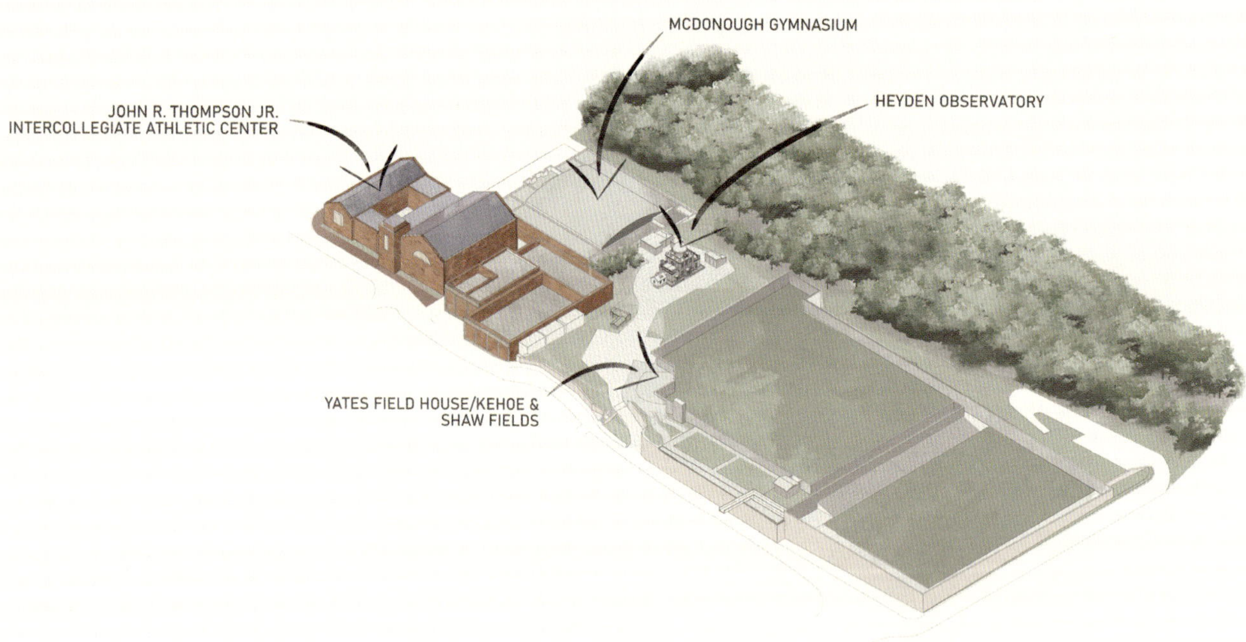
MCDONOUGH GYMNASIUM
JOHN R. THOMPSON JR.
INTERCOLLEGIATE ATHLETIC CENTER
HEYDEN OBSERVATORY
YATES FIELD HOUSE/KEHOE &
SHAW FIELDS

Area VII

West Campus: Sports and Observatory

The earliest structure in this western section of campus is the mid-nineteenth-century Heyden Observatory (1844), which rests on a hill overlooking the university. Although now hemmed in by the heating and cooling plant, McDonough Gymnasium (1952), and Yates Field House (1979), in the Heyden Observatory's early years, a vineyard and cow pasture surrounded the small pioneering building. In the mid-twentieth century, construction of the McDonough Gymnasium gave the university new and ample athletic space, replacing the small gym previously located within what is now the Davis Performing Arts Center. Also within this west campus area is Kehoe Field, above Yates Field House, and Shaw Field, which extends further to the north toward the medical center. By building the multipurpose Yates Field House largely under Kehoe Field via the use of an innovative interior vaulting system, the facilities intruded on only a minor portion of precious campus space. Most recently, in 2016 Georgetown's newest athletic center, commemorating celebrated basketball coach John R. Thompson Jr. (1941–2020), opened just to the east of McDonough Gym. The John R. Thompson Jr. Intercollegiate Athletic Center received LEED gold certification.

Astronomical Observatory, Georgetown College D.C. J. A. Simpson, engraved by H. Weber, nineteenth century. (Georgetown University Art Collection)

Georgetown University, Washington, D. C., The Observatory. Postcard ca. 1950. (Georgetown University Archives)

McDonough Memorial Gymnasium. Photograph by William Beanland, 1951. (Georgetown University Archives)

McDonough Gymnasium (1952)

McDonough Gymnasium, located south of the Heyden Observatory on the campus's far west side, opened in 1952. McDonough replaced Ryan Gymnasium, which had served the university well when the college's enrollment hovered around one hundred students. The old gym's inadequacies in hosting an increasing number of students and its structural deficiencies prompted the creation of plans for a new gym by the 1930s. However, World War II intervened. During the war, significant military training programs occurred on campus. Immediately after the war, the construction of the Georgetown University Hospital took precedence, and not until 1947 did attention refocus on the need for a new athletics center. Originally slated to be constructed next to Ryan Gymnasium near the campus's historic core, due to noise, parking, and access issues the McDonough Gymnasium's site shifted west.

In the years following the war, the university lacked surplus funds for a gym's construction. There was an immediate need of $800,000 to construct the facility, and the Alumni Association and students led the efforts to raise the money for the new building. The Alumni Association organized a nationwide fundraising drive headed by Charles J. Milton (C 1935). Contributing industry leaders realized that the improvement of educational

McDonough Memorial Gymnasium.

institutions played an important role in developing future strong business leaders. The cost of the new gymnasium amounted to $1.25 million.

The gym commemorates Vincent Stanislaus McDonough, SJ (1870–1939), who came to Georgetown in 1916. McDonough served as athletic director from 1916 to 1928 and later in various student-advising roles. The expansive arena provides seating for some twenty-five hundred fans and frequently hosts university events, including graduation ceremonies. Among other sports, the women's basketball and volleyball teams practice and play here. Several significant events have been held at the McDonough Gymnasium since its 1952 opening, including an inaugural ball for President Dwight Eisenhower as well as concerts by the Grateful Dead, Count Basie, and Bruce Springsteen. The men's basketball team played games at McDonough prior to moving to the Capital Centre in Maryland in the early 1980s and later to the Capital One Arena in downtown Washington, DC.

Prominent local architect Leon Chatelain (1902–79) designed the gymnasium using red brick, Indiana limestone, and reinforced concrete. Born in Washington, DC, Chatelain attended night classes in architecture at George Washington University. He spent time working as a draftsman for Waddy B. Wood before opening his own practice in the 1930s. Chatelain had a long-standing relationship with the C&P Telephone Company and designed its headquarters in 1948. Among Chatelain's other notable Washington-area buildings are the Westmoreland Congregational Church (1948–55), the Editors Building (Hampton Inn) (1949–50), and the former

McDonough Memorial Gymnasium under construction. Reni Newsphoto Service, ca. 1951. (Georgetown University Archives)

Fannie Mae Headquarters (now a mixed-use residential development on Wisconsin Avenue) (1956–58). On the Georgetown campus, Chatelain also designed Saint Mary's Hall.

Chatelain's work varied, but he often employed the Colonial Revival and Stripped Classical architectural styles. A field leader, Chatelain served as the American Institute of Architects president from 1956 to 1958 and led in the effort for accessible building design. The architect's son, Leon Chatelain III, took over his father's practice and continued to run what became one of the oldest architectural firms continuously in operation in the District of Columbia. The Chatelain firm merged with Bowie Gridley Architects in 2011.

Heavy and imposing, McDonough Gymnasium's symmetry and arched roof, as well as the shields installed above the front doors, lend the structure a sense of grandeur. Despite the cohesive campus-friendly brick, the Stripped Classical style manifests in the gym's arched entranceway divided by weighty brick pilasters and a sharp, flat roofline above. This Stripped Classical mode sets the gym apart from other campus buildings. It is notable that Waddy Wood's earlier Department of the Interior building (1936) exemplifies this style. John McShain (1898–1989), who attended Georgetown, led the gymnasium's construction. Well-known for his building work throughout the nation's capital, McShain worked on such notable sites as the Kennedy Center, the Pentagon, and a White House renovation.

—GS & SR

Bus stop near McDonough Memorial Gymnasium.

John R. Thompson Jr. Intercollegiate Athletic Center (2016)

Georgetown's newest intercollegiate athletic center, named after celebrated basketball coach John Thompson Jr. (1941–2020), opened in 2016. Thompson coached the men's basketball team from 1972 to 1999, leading them to three NCAA Final Four Tournaments and the 1984 National Championship win. With nearly six hundred victories to his credit, Thompson had the most wins of any Hoyas basketball coach. A bronze statue of Thompson dominates the athletic complex's lobby.

Located adjacent to McDonough Gymnasium, the Thompson Athletic Center was designed by the local firm of Bowie Gridley, along with the global Populous company; Whiting-Turner Contracting constructed the complex. Prior to the Thompson Athletic Center's appearance, tennis courts resided on the site. This mammoth facility replaced McDonough Gym as the university's primary athletic complex. In 1952, when McDonough opened, there were some 250 student-athletes competing in nine varsity sports at the university. Now, some thirty Georgetown varsity sports programs and close to 800 student-athletes use the Thompson facility.

The five-story brick and limestone trim complex includes roughly 144,000 square feet of space. The $60 million structure houses practice courts, staff offices, team meeting rooms, a sports medicine center, and locker rooms.

John R. Thompson Jr. Intercollegiate Athletic Center.

Weight training areas, study space, the Georgetown Athletic Hall of Fame, and a courtyard are also found within the center.

The two brick structures—McDonough Gym and the Thompson Center—connect on McDonough's eastern side. As a result of the intentional use of brick and limestone trim on the Thompson Center, visually the two buildings transition smoothly, with the new complex running perpendicular to the old. The Thompson Center's design evolved and responded to feedback from the Old Georgetown Board. In 2011 this group criticized some early designs for the structure, claiming they were awkward and looked too much like a dormitory. The architects removed a planned glass wall as well as a wing that would have somewhat obstructed the view of the earlier gym. Today the Thompson Center presents a bold street facade. From Yates Walk, north of the complex's projecting central entranceway, a colossal lunette window rests above a bank of bold rectangular fenestration. The building's north and south limestone-lined roofs echo the many sharp pediments found throughout campus.

Heyden Observatory (1844)

Heyden Observatory emerged during the tenure of Georgetown president James Ryder, SJ (1840–45 and 1848–51), who sought to make science integral to the curriculum. It was, however, the work of James Curley, SJ (1796–1889) that launched construction of the Observatory. Originally from Ireland, Curley in 1831 began a more-than-fifty-year Georgetown career, teaching physics, botany, chemistry, and astronomy. Curley served as the Observatory's first director; he also selected the building's site, designed its structure, and ordered its early scientific instruments from Europe. Given the costs involved, the Jesuits in Rome were not supportive of Curley's project; however, due to miscommunication and the time lag of mail delivery, the building succeeded under Curley's passionate aegis.

The Observatory's site was truly a place apart from the central academic buildings. Located on an elevated ridge, the 1852 *Annals of the Observatory* note that the building was to be "about 400 yards 70 degrees NW from the College." To the north a cow pasture occupied the adjacent land. Highlighting this rural landscape, former Observatory director Francis Heyden, SJ, described the 1840s campus as "mostly a farm with its cows, giving their fresh milk to the growing boys in the dormitory, chickens stalking all over and vineyards for altar wine." In stark contrast, today's view of the campus from Observatory hill highlights Georgetown's minimal green spaces and the challenge of meeting the needs of a twenty-first-century university on a landlocked site.

Although the Observatory now appears like a relic of a lost era, it was a leading institution for both its structure and the research its inhabitants

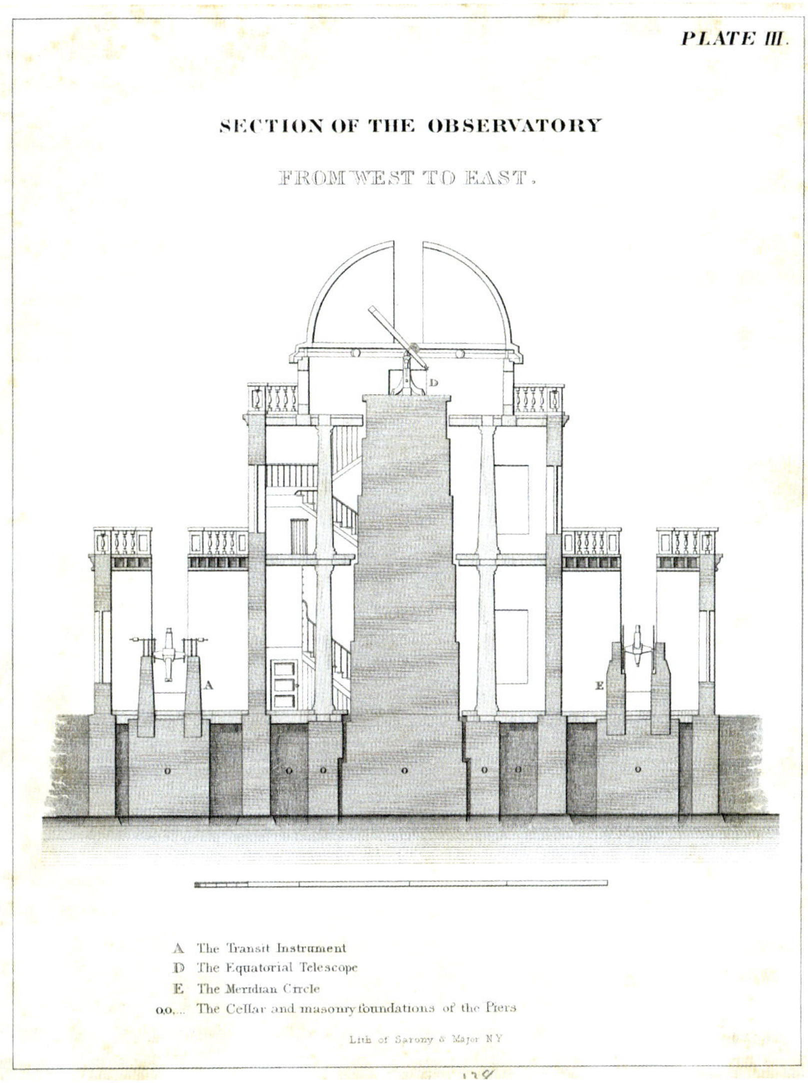

Section of the Heyden Observatory, From *Annals of the Astronomical Observatory of Georgetown College*, plate 3. (Georgetown University Archives)

produced. One of the earliest college observatories in the country, by the end of the 1840s only three other colleges—North Carolina, Williams, and Western Reserve—had built similar small observatories. Moreover, in 1846 Curley, working together with local and English scientists, used the building's instruments to calculate the longitude and latitude of the Observatory and other important DC sites such as the Washington Monument, the White House, the Capitol, and the Smithsonian Institution. Such measurements were pioneering for the time.

Designed expressly to house a telescope, a meridian circle, and transit-measuring instruments, the carefully aligned building is 60 feet long and about 30 feet wide. The ground floor contains three rooms: The east and west rooms are one story and 15 feet high. The Observatory's high central domed

OPPOSITE: Heyden Observatory.

section houses the telescope. Painted white, a balustrade caps each of the three sections; tin once covered the Observatory roof. Stone piers formed the supporting base for the Observatory's instruments, which rested under interior ceilings painted sky blue.

The construction of the US Naval Observatory in the city's Foggy Bottom neighborhood was contemporaneous with the building of the university's observatory. Emphasizing the connection between the two buildings, the *Annals of the Astronomical Observatory* noted that the Naval Observatory was located precisely 56 degrees southeast and 8,764 feet from Georgetown's observatory. Though smaller than the government building, with its domed central section and two lower wings, the Georgetown structure echoes that of the US Navy.

Two Jesuits provided the seed funds for the building and instruments. Emmett Curran, in his history of Georgetown University, highlights that the development of the Observatory was typical of the private character of the astronomy "movement" in antebellum America. In 1841 Br. Thomas Meredith Jenkins, prevented from pursuing his goal of becoming an astronomer due to his poor health, offered $8,000 from his estate, while Charles Stonestreet, SJ (Georgetown president 1851–52) provided $2,000 toward the cost of the instruments. Ultimately the Observatory cost roughly $9,000 to build and the equipment likely close to $18,000.

During the nineteenth century multiple European Jesuit scientists and mathematicians had important connections with the Observatory. The Italian Benedict Sestini (1816–90) was active at Georgetown for some twenty years and published math textbooks, while the Jesuit astronomer and pioneer in astrophysics Angelo Secchi (1818–78) worked briefly at the Observatory. After Curley's tenure, John Hagen, SJ, and later Paul A. McNally, SJ, directed the Observatory, producing research on stars and solar eclipses. Father Francis J. Heyden led the Observatory from 1948 to 1972, an important period for the observatory, with eclipse expeditions and innovative astronomical research. By the 1970s, however, light pollution negatively impacted the Observatory's effectiveness, and the building closed in 1972. In 1987 the university dedicated the Observatory and its surrounding gardens to Heyden. The Heyden Observatory is listed on the National Register of Historic Places.

Yates Field House (1979)

Completed in 1979, the Yates Field House honors Gerard F. Yates, SJ, who spent forty years at Georgetown as a professor of government, dean of the graduate school, and director of international student programs. Located north of the Observatory on the west side of Yates Walk, this multipurpose athletic center sits largely underneath Kehoe Field. By building the structure

Yates Field House.

beneath the athletic field, essentially unseen, the university conserved campus space and avoided lengthy design reviews by neighborhood boards and the city's Commission on Fine Arts. Among the many elements included within Yates's belowground space is a swimming and diving pool; multiple basketball and tennis courts; an indoor track; squash, racquetball, and handball courts; batting and golf areas; cardio and weight training spaces; and a dance studio.

Developed during the presidency of Timothy Healy, SJ, in the 1970s, Yates Field House was one solution to the university's lack of indoor recreational space for students. At the time, intercollegiate basketball and volleyball were among the few sports the McDonough Gym served. Federal regulations mandating equal athletic facilities for men and women also prompted Yates's development.

Swimming pool in Yates Field House, 1980. (Georgetown University Archives)

Architect and structural engineer Daniel F. Tully designed the 142,000-square-foot facility. Tully attended the Massachusetts Institute of Technology and Auburn University and designed athletic facilities for many US universities, including Boston College and Brown University. Along with these campus commissions, over the course of his career Tully built many places of worship in New England. Celebrated for his engineering innovation, Tully also helped to stabilize Pisa's leaning tower during repairs to the historic structure.

Tully employed his hallmark "hyperbolic parabolic" ceiling arches in the field house. These arches look like colossal inverted umbrellas in undulating patterns. The innovative system enabled Tully to create a wide-open gym space with few support columns. The hyperbolic parabolic design, for which

Tully obtained a patent, incorporated a metal and concrete structural layer above the triangular arches, which supports the Kehoe athletic field above.

Dating back to 1942, this field house name commemorates John Kehoe, Georgetown's athletic director from 1932 to 1944. The university razed the field in 1976 to make room for Yates Field House. After the field reopened in 1979, it faced persistent structural problems. Drainage issues and splitting turf compromised the field's level playing surface and led to repeated repairs in the following years.

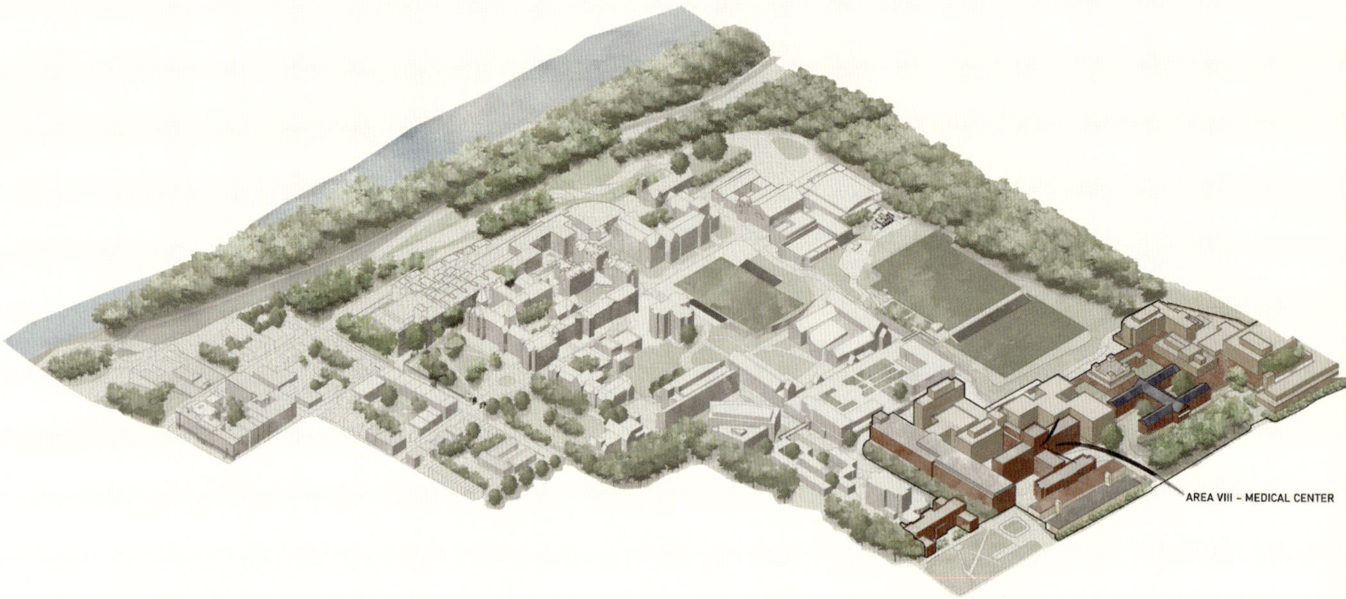
AREA VIII – MEDICAL CENTER

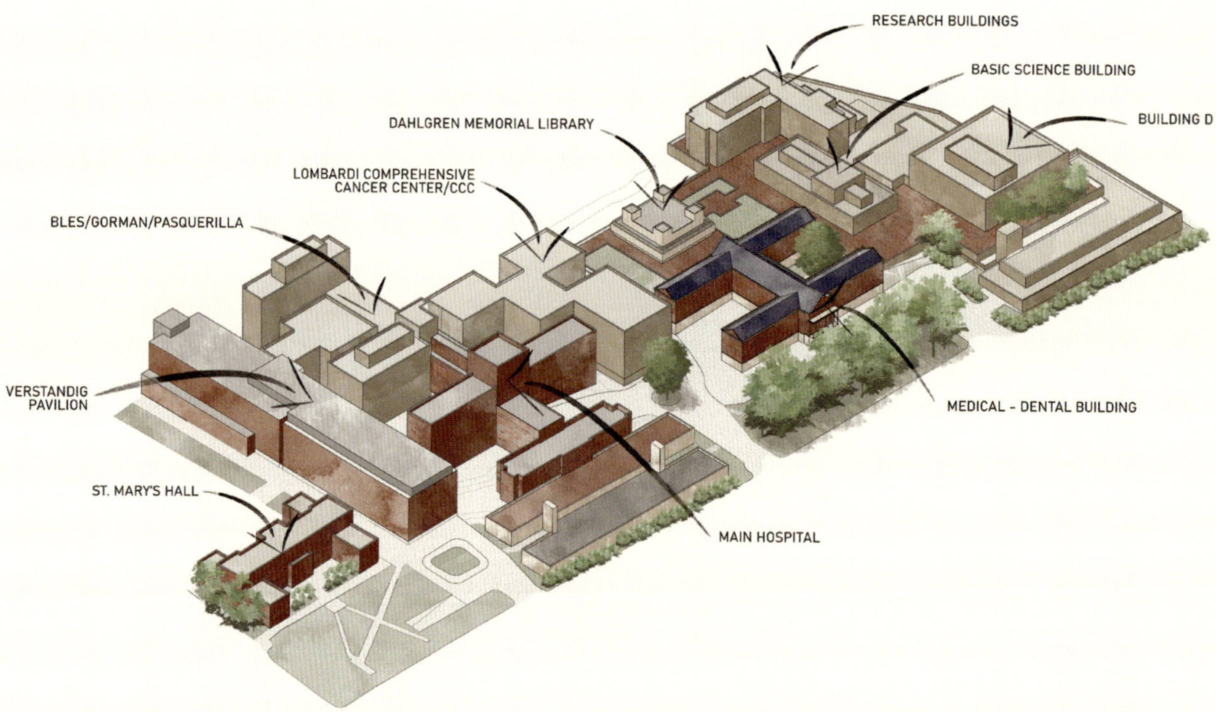
RESEARCH BUILDINGS
BASIC SCIENCE BUILDING
DAHLGREN MEMORIAL LIBRARY
BUILDING D
LOMBARDI COMPREHENSIVE CANCER CENTER/CCC
BLES/GORMAN/PASQUERILLA
VERSTANDIG PAVILION
MEDICAL - DENTAL BUILDING
ST. MARY'S HALL
MAIN HOSPITAL

Area VIII

Medical Center

A complex of buildings on the northwest edge of the main campus, bounded by Reservoir Road on the north, makes up the Georgetown Medical Center. In 1849 four Washington, DC, physicians—Noble Young, Charles Liberman, Johnson Eliot, and Flodoardo Howard—approached James Ryder, SJ, president of Georgetown University, asking to establish a college of medicine. At that time the only other teaching institution in Washington was the Medical Department at Columbian College (which later became the medical school at George Washington University). Georgetown's Department of Medicine first resided in a warehouse on F Street near the corner of 12th Street; the founding doctors set up two lecture rooms, a room for practical anatomy, and an infirmary. From the inaugural class of eight students in 1850, enrollment steadily increased, partly spurred by the need for medical professionals to treat Civil War wounded. The program relocated a few times to accommodate continuing growth. In 1869 the medicine faculty leased a new space on 10th and E Streets. In 1886 the department moved into its own facility—a two-story structure at 920 H Street NW. By 1893 the addition of a third story and extension of the building walls effectively doubled the size of the school.

Medical-Dental Building (1930)

The gradual modernization of medical training in the early twentieth century raised the College of Medicine's profile at the university. The university made plans to move what began as a largely autonomous unit to the main campus, and in 1930 the School of Medicine relocated to its current home, the Medical-Dental Building. The brick Colonial Revival structure, originally consisting of three stories and an attic, was laid out in a H-shaped plan meant to minimize the distance between laboratories and classrooms. The long wings housed laboratories; the connecting wing contained lecture

OL OF MEDICINE
SCHOOL OF DENTISTRY

Medical Campus: Medical-Dental Building, Concentrated Care Center, and the Dahlgren Memorial Library.

Medical-Dental Building. (Georgetown University Archives)

halls and an amphitheater. The facade featured repeating rows of windows on each level, punctuated at intervals by stonework on the ground level and classical columns spanning the second and third stories. A triangular pediment crowned the center of the long axis.

Georgetown University Hospital (1948)

The four doctors who originated the Georgetown Department of Medicine in 1850 did not have access to National Hospital, at that time the only such facility in the city, since it was restricted to the Columbian College medicine faculty. This was one of the reasons they approached the university to start their own medical school. The infirmary, in its first incarnation on F Street, consisted of six beds and a dispensary for treating the sick poor. The Georgetown doctors gradually formed affiliations with other hospitals in the area. Providence, Emergency, Garfield, and Children's Hospitals were among the network of facilities that provided medical students with essential field training. The growing emphasis on clinical experience was one factor that led to Georgetown building the first university hospital in 1898, on N Street between 35th and 36th Street, to the east of the main campus entrance. The four-story structure had thirty-three beds when it opened; by 1927 there were close to three hundred.

A 1940 survey determined that in a war emergency Washington, DC, would require 1,500 more hospital beds in addition to the 3,735 it already had. Major funding for the present-day Georgetown University Hospital came from the Lanham Act of 1944, which provided grants through the Federal Works Administration. President Franklin Delano Roosevelt approved a grant of $3.6 million for the building, which was later dedicated in his honor. In 1948 the new 407-bed hospital opened on Reservoir Road, adjacent to the Medical-Dental Building. Together the two buildings form the core of the Medical Complex. The mid-twentieth-century blocky and spare hospital building is seven stories high, made of reinforced concrete with brick curtain walls and stone trim. An eighth story houses building service equipment. At its highest peak a great cross stands in relief against the masonry. Lower, brick rectangular building sections and a concrete parking garage are located to the north, adjacent to the hospital's central mass. The garage and the site's rising grade make the hospital building difficult to view from Reservoir Road.

In the later twentieth century, multiple substantial buildings were added to the early hospital's footprint. In 1959 the university added the Gorman Building on the south side. Dedicated to past Georgetown president Lawrence Gorman, SJ (1942–49), the Gorman Building added diagnostic, treatment, and research spaces. Later, in 1972, Mariani and Associates designed the Marcus J. Bles Building on the southeastern corner. This brick-and-concrete structure commemorates Marcus Bles, who came to the Washington, DC, area from Missouri and rose to become a successful

Garden between the Medical-Dental Building and the Concentrated Care Center.

land investor. Bles and his family received medical care at the Georgetown Hospital, and in gratitude donated land in Loudoun County, Virginia, to the university. In 1977 the Chicago-based firm of Perkins&Will added to the structure.

Located to the east of the early Medical-Dental Building, the pioneering Concentrated Care Center (CCC) arose in 1976. The CCC was over a decade in planning, due largely to funding delays. Nonetheless, at its opening the building was one of the most advanced facilities in the country for acute illness and disaster care. Architects Metcalfe & Associates created the CCC's final design and the federal government funded the majority of the over $20 million cost for construction. The CCC includes innovative care units configured with central medical stations surrounded by patient rooms.

During the 1980s the university added two additional structures to the hospital complex. Perkins&Will designed the Lombardi Comprehensive Cancer Center, located to the south of the CCC. Opening in 1982, the modern Lombardi Center commemorates the celebrated football coach of the Green Bay Packers and Washington Commanders Vincent T. Lombardi, who had been a cancer patient at Georgetown. The Lombardi Center's glass southern facade wall, bold cantilevered entrance awning, and soaring open

Lombardi Comprehensive Cancer Center interior.

interior atrium provide a vibrant, modern addition to the medical complex. Further south within the hospital's grounds is the Pasquerilla Health Center, designed by Martin Reddy Architects and added in 1988. The building commemorates its funding patrons, Frank and Sylvia Pasquerilla of Pennsylvania.

The university recently added the transformative Verstandig Pavilion along the eastern side of the medical complex. Designed by Shalom Baranes Associates, the 477,000-square-foot complex provides a new

Verstandig Pavilion detail.

Emergency Department, more than 150 patient rooms, and 31 operating rooms. Featuring a streamlined exterior design composed of twenty-eight thousand terra-cotta pieces and nearly a thousand windows, the rectangular pavilion covers much of what had been open parking space between the hospital and Saint Mary's Hall. The building's flat roofline echoes the lines of the older hospital building to the west. Open green space with trees and walkways fronts Saint Mary's Hall and surrounds the pavilion on its north-east side along Reservoir Road. The pavilion also includes three levels of underground parking, with over six hundred spaces.

Saint Mary's Hall (1956)

Saint Mary's Hall, located on Reservoir Road to the east of the hospital, opened in 1956 and is the third-oldest building in the medical complex, after the Medical-Dental Building and the hospital. Today it houses the Georgetown School of Nursing and the Georgetown School of Health as well as the Computer Science and Math Departments. However, it was originally designed as the teaching facility for the nursing program and as a dormitory for the program's students. The Georgetown Training School for Nurses (later the School of Nursing) was founded in 1903. A nurse's "education" consisted of working in the hospital wards affiliated with the university. Gradually this would change and trend toward a more structured curriculum that involved formal classroom sessions and well-defined nursing specializations.

The United States' entry into World War II fueled a demand for more nurses. From the nursing school's perspective this required scaling up its capacity to house nursing students. In 1943 the university procured federal funding to build the first Saint Mary's Hall, a dormitory for seventy-five student nurses, at 35th and Prospect Streets. Today this is the site of Loyola/Xavier/Ryder Hall. The construction of the new university hospital on Reservoir Road in 1947 freed up the old hospital building on 35th and N Streets to include additional nursing dormitories.

The Hospital Survey and Construction Act of 1946, otherwise known as the Hill-Burton Act after its US Senate sponsors, provided funds for building community hospitals. The university applied for and received financial assistance to build a new nursing school and dormitory—the current Saint Mary's Hall—near the hospital on Reservoir Road. Dedicated in 1956, the building was of light red brick trimmed with limestone on a four-story central portion flanked by three-story wings, each featuring a niche for religious sculpture. The first floor housed four study rooms, a 240-capacity auditorium, a chapel with seating for 200, and a dining hall that could serve 200. The upper floors contained rooms for 210 students and faculty. The architect,

Saint Mary's Building with the Hospital and Medical-Dental Building behind. Darrell C. Crain Photographic Collection, 1958. (Courtesy The People's Archive, DC Public Library)

Basic Science Building.

Leon Chatelain, also designed the McDonough Gymnasium, a structure whose prominent pillars framing the entrance and graceful roofline and ground floor curves relieve its pronounced horizontality. By contrast, Saint Mary's Hall was boxy and flat-roofed, reflecting the spare, modular "Hill-Burton" aesthetic mandated for most federally funded buildings in the 1950s.

Saint Mary's Hall was state of the art for its time; it was the first building at the university to have air conditioning. However, by the 1990s the teaching and dormitory space configuration was outmoded. In 1996 the university closed three student residence floors due to safety concerns. A major renovation in 2001–2 transformed the interior of Saint Mary's into a state-of-the art facility boasting medical diagnostic simulation programs, along with student social and collaborative meeting spaces.

Today, to the west of Saint Mary's Hall and the hospital, the Medical-Dental Building provides the architectural focal point of the medical structures amid an array of later modernist boxes. The Brutalist mass of the John Vinton Dahlgren Memorial Library (1971) across from the Medical-Dental Building provides an interesting visual juxtaposition and gestures to the growth of the complex in the late twentieth century. Gardens and a courtyard counterbalance the library's weighty hovering concrete.

Along with Dahlgren Library, architects Frank Ellerbe and Mariani designed other office and research buildings along the western edge of the medical complex in the early 1970s. These boxy, three-story, flat-roofed structures are largely composed of wide brick and concrete bands, which make a material visual connection to the flagship, Depression-era Medical-Dental Building.

—NA & SR

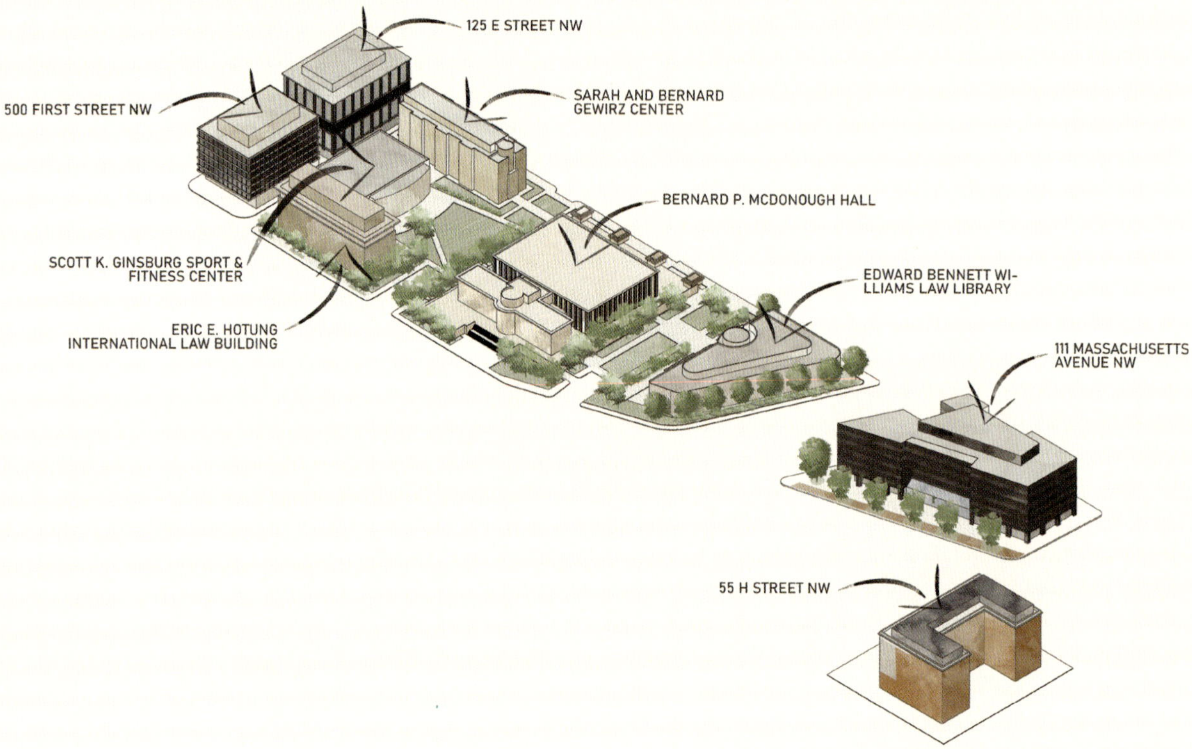
125 E STREET NW
500 FIRST STREET NW
SARAH AND BERNARD GEWIRZ CENTER
BERNARD P. MCDONOUGH HALL
SCOTT K. GINSBURG SPORT & FITNESS CENTER
EDWARD BENNETT WILLIAMS LAW LIBRARY
ERIC E. HOTUNG INTERNATIONAL LAW BUILDING
111 MASSACHUSETTS AVENUE NW
55 H STREET NW

Area IX

Law Center and Capitol Campus

Law Center (1971 plus)

Always situated outside the confines of the main campus, the Georgetown Law Center began its life in the 1870s. In 1891, it moved to its fifth site in the first university-owned building at 506 E Street, near Judiciary Square. This was home to the Law Center until 1971, when it relocated to the Bernard P. McDonough Hall on New Jersey Avenue. The center's original entrance sign at Judiciary Square today sits within the Quad.

Noted midcentury modernist architect Edward Durell Stone designed McDonough Hall around the same time as his most famous Washington, DC, landmark design, the John F. Kennedy Center for the Performing Arts. Both structures exemplify the stripped down Classical idiom that Stone favored: a rectangular mass of concrete and glass set upon a pedestal and spanned by attenuated vertical elements. Stone's buildings appear as modern temples, the Kennedy Center to the arts and McDonough Hall to the law. At the Law Center, however, budget constraints eliminated significant marble in favor of buff brick.

While the press lauded Stone's structure for its iconicity, they criticized its rather uninspired internal plan. The burgeoning Law Center also outgrew the McDonough Hall in short order, and in 1983 the university engaged the DC firm of Hartman-Cox Architects to expand the campus perimeter with new buildings. The Edward Bennett Williams Law Library (1989), the Bernard and Sarah Gewirz Student Center (1993), and the extension to McDonough Hall (1997) all took a visual cue from the classicism of the initial building, echoing its scale and materials but varying the rhythm of structural elements and decorative motifs. The resulting complex of buildings added much-needed and better-functioning space, while respectfully referencing the historic legacy of McDonough yet alleviating what some thought to be the severity of the original design.

Bernard P. McDonough Hall.

Law Center Sign from early E Street entrance.

McDonough Hall at the Law Center, designed by Edward Durell Stone, 1985. (Georgetown University Archives)

Edward Bennett Williams Law Library.

Law Center—Scott K. Ginsburg Sport & Fitness Center.

125 E Street NW. To the right is 500 First Street NW.

Additional buildings on the law campus opened in 2004. The Eric E. Hotung International Law Center includes state-of-the-art classrooms and a mock-up of the US Supreme Court's chambers. The Scott K. Ginsburg Sport & Fitness Center has a basketball court, a four-lane 25-meter pool, exercise facilities, and a café and lounge. The Boston architectural firm of Shepley Bulfinch Richardson & Abbott designed both buildings.

—NA & SR

Capitol Campus

Just a few blocks north of the US Capitol Building and west of Union Station, the buildings composing the Capitol Campus include 125 E Street, 500 First Street, 55 H Street, and 111 Massachusetts Avenue. All the Capitol Campus buildings are within close proximity to the Law Center, which sits at the center of this campus.

125 E Street (2024)

The 125 E Street building opened in 2024. It shares a city block with the Law Center and connects on its eastern side with the 500 First Street building. The E Street building houses the McCourt School of Public Policy and serves as an anchor for the downtown campus. Designed by Robert A. M. Stern Architects, this light-filled modern building with perfectly positioned views of the Capitol possesses a rectangular footprint and stands at the corner of E and 2nd Streets. The structure includes nine floors and rises to a flat roof, with a slightly projecting eastern side. The exterior of 125 E Street, particularly its long, south elevation, presents a rhythmic, geometric patchwork of glass, metal cladding, pilasters of varied heights and widths, and contrasting light-hued stone. The light stone, pierced by rectangular windows, ascends the south facade's eastern side in a stepped configuration. Abstract colossal pilasters join the building's central and uppermost stories. Sharp horizontal shades hang atop long rectangular windows and heighten the building's exterior cadence. Along with classroom and office space, the 125 E Street interior boasts a soaring lobby area, a four-hundred-seat auditorium, and multiple social and convening spaces. In addition, celebrated architect and designer Maya Lin (b. 1959) created multiple luminous art installations for 125 E Street.

Lin's work connects with the natural environment. Pendant, dove-like lights shift in color based on exterior weather changes and animate 125 E Street's lobby and stairway areas. In addition, Lin designed a sprawling ceiling installation inspired by the Potomac River's tributaries, composed of glimmering, aqua-hued translucent marbles. Also by Lin is an oval metal bench above the upper causeway between 125 E Street and 500 First Street surrounded by dramatic sky views. Lin's art, combined with RAMSA's inclusion of ample open space, an interior white palette, and clear framing of exterior views, creates an ethereal sensation in areas of this Georgetown building.

Along with 125 E Street, RAMSA also designed the building at 55 H Street and in its geometric exterior patterning and transparent glass, the two buildings share affinity. An architectural firm integral to the university's twenty-first-century development, RAMSA has designed

OPPOSITE: 125 E Street NW, south elevation.

multiple Georgetown buildings in recent years, including the main campus's Southwest Quadrangle 2003, the Leo J. O'Donovan Dining Hall (2003), and the new Henle Village (2025). Stern is a leading figure in American architecture and served as the dean of the Yale School of Architecture for many years. Founded in 1969 and based in New York City, RAMSA has a strong international reputation in residential, commercial, and institutional work, with a list of other higher-education clients that includes Harvard University, the University of Connecticut, Colgate University, Villanova University, and the University of Virginia. The firm often employs a modern traditionalist style that exhibits a reverence for the past.

500 First Street (1969)

To the east of 125 E Street stands 500 First Street. Originally built in 1969 and acquired by the university in 2019, this nine-story Brutalist-style concrete structure possesses a compact rectangular footprint. Resting on a slightly smaller two-story base, the building's long southern E Street elevation has four wide uniform bays. Rectangular single-pane windows set within recessed concrete frames mark the building's upper seven stories. On its eastern side, a glass entranceway projects onto First Street, while walkways connect the building to 125 E Street on its western side. With over 130,000 square feet of space, this structure provides a mixture of classrooms, offices, and collaboration areas for interdisciplinary programs. Students in Georgetown's Capitol Applied Learning Labs Program use 500 First Street as well as 55 H Street, as the program requires that they spend a semester living, studying, and working in downtown DC.

55 H Street (2022)

Located just a few blocks northeast of 125 E Street, the 55 H Street apartment-style residence opened in 2022 and provides housing for over 450 undergraduate and graduate students. RAMSA worked with American Campus Communities, a Texas-based developer of student housing facilities, to develop 55 H Street. The building possesses an extended U-shaped footprint, with its south facade lining H Street. The building's geometric exterior employs a dynamic mixture of elements, including thin red brick columns on the lower stories, buff brick panels above, and red brick on the sides. Metal, glass, and integrated solar panels mark 55 H Street's upper stories. The building's largely transparent ground floor forges a connection to the surrounding site and street. The buff brick and light stone gestures to the nearby Law Center's exterior hues, while its red brick echoes the surrounding historic neighborhood structures, including the large-scale Romanesque Revival–style Government Printing Office (1903) across H Street.

55 H Street NW.

Along with apartment-style housing, 55 H Street includes many student amenities. Similar to the main campus's Healey Family Student Center, the interior common space includes a green wall as well as a fireplace, creating a living room–like setting, and several open flexible seating areas and closed study rooms. The residence has an open rear courtyard for outdoor eating, while the upper floors provide broad city views. This Capitol Campus building achieved LEED platinum certification and in 2023 received awards from Student Housing Business in the categories of Green and Sustainable Construction and Architecture and Design.

111 Massachusetts Avenue (1983)

The university purchased 111 Massachusetts Avenue in 2021. Leading Washington architect Vlastimil Koubek (1927–2003) designed this eight-story mammoth building, which resides across the street from the law library. Occupying a full city block, 111 Massachusetts Avenue sits with H Street to the north, Massachusetts Avenue to the south, 2nd Street to the west, and New Jersey Avenue to the east. Built in 1983 and popularly dubbed the "Darth Vader" building, Koubek's structure possesses a smooth, dark glass and black stone exterior with razor-sharp angled corners. In the form of an irregular quadrilateral, central indentations mark the building's east, west, and south sides, while hulking southern piers and a flat northern elevation anchor its over 300,000 square feet of space.

Born in Brno, Czech Republic, Koubek came to the United States in 1952. After working briefly in New York City with the leading architectural firm of Emery Roth and Sons, Koubek opened his own firm in Washington, DC, in 1957. A prolific designer and one of DC's most influential architects, Koubek created designs for more than one hundred buildings, most in the nation's capital. Koubek's office, hotel, and apartment buildings together have had a tremendous impact on the city's skyline. Frequently employing a sleek modernist style, Koubek designed many of the city's early "glass box" buildings. The Brawner Building in Farragut Square, 1325 and 1625 Massachusetts Avenue, the Fairmont Hotel on M Street, the L'Enfant Plaza Hotel, and the International Square Building on K Street are among Koubek's many DC buildings. Along with his modernist structures, Koubek also renovated the Willard Hotel.

For many years the 111 Massachusetts Avenue building housed the Union Labor Life Insurance Company. In 2002 Douglas Development purchased the building. The SmithGroup architecture and engineering firm, and its contractor, Whiting-Turner, are part of the development team currently renovating 111 Massachusetts Avenue. New entrances, new transparent glass ribbon windows, and greenery on the rooftop and streetscape are among the planned building updates. Upon completion this Capitol Campus building will host a range of academic fields and interdisciplinary programs.

OPPOSITE: 111 Massachusetts Avenue NW.

SPEED
LIMIT

Notes

INTRODUCTION

1 Rachel Swarns, *The 272: The Families Who Were Enslaved and Sold to Build the American Catholic Church* (New York: Random House, 2023), 22.
2 Paul R. O'Neill and Paul K. Williams, *Georgetown University* (Charleston: Arcadia, 2003), 11–12.
3 Paul Venable Turner, *Campus: An American Planning Tradition* (Cambridge: MIT Press), 47–48.
4 Robert Emmett Curran, *A History of Georgetown University: From Academy to University*, vol. 1 (Washington, DC: Georgetown University Press, 2010), 359.
5 Grace Ring, Georgetown University student Col '21, spring 2020.
6 "The College Walks," *Georgetown College Journal* 1, no. 8 (October 1873): 1.
7 Juliana Brint, "Six Feet Under," *Georgetown Voice*, March 26, 2019, 1–2.
8 Elsa Barraza Mendoza, "Catholic Slave Owners and the Development of Georgetown University's Slave Hiring System, 1792–1862," in *Facing Georgetown's History: A Reader on Slavery, Memory and Reconciliation*, ed. Adam Rothman and Elsa Mendoza (Washington, DC: Georgetown University Press, 2021), 59–63, 67.
9 Georgetown University, *Report of the Working Group on Slavery, Memory, and Reconciliation* (Washington, DC: Georgetown University, 2016), 17, 23, 101–2.
10 Adam Rothman and students, "The Price of Georgetown—White-Gravenor Hall," Georgetown University, summer 2020, https://slaveryarchive.georgetown.edu/items/show/505.
11 O'Neill and Williams, *Georgetown University*, 31, 36.
12 Hardy George, "Georgetown University's Healy Building," *Journal of the Society of Architectural Historians* 31, no. 3 (October 1972): 208–16.
13 Adam Rothman and Elsa Mendoza, eds., *Facing Georgetown's History: A Reader on Slavery, Memory and Reconciliation* (Washington, DC: Georgetown University Press, 2021), 2.
14 Benjamin Henry Latrobe, "Plan of the West End," *Histories of the National Mall*, accessed September 7, 2023, https://mallhistory.org/items/show/399.

15 Turner, *Campus*, 57–61, 62–67.

16 Turner, *Campus*, 38.

17 Robert Emmett Curran, *A History of Georgetown University, the Quest for Excellence*, vol. 2 (Washington, DC: Georgetown University Press, 2020), 147.

18 Thomas J. Shelley, *Fordham, A History of the Jesuit University of New York: 1841–2003* (New York: Fordham University Press, 2016), 174.

19 Rothman and Mendoza, *Facing Georgetown's History*, 313.

20 Dale Allen Gyure, "The Heart of the University: A History of the Library as an Architectural Symbol of American Higher Education," *Winterthur Portfolio* 42 (Summer-Autumn 2008): 107–32.

21 Carla Yanni, *Living on Campus: An Architectural History of the American Dormitory* (Minneapolis: University of Minnesota Press, 2019), 8, 31.

Bibliography

Frequently Referenced Works

Ballman, Francis X. *Building Outlines: Campus Buildings, 1789–1995*. Washington, DC: Georgetown University Archives, 1995.

BFCSC/GUA. Booth Family Center for Special Collections. Georgetown University Archives, Lauinger Library.

Curran, Robert Emmett. *A History of Georgetown University*. Vol. 1, *From Academy to University, 1789–1889*. Washington, DC: Georgetown University Press, 2010.

———. *A History of Georgetown University*. Vol. 2, *The Quest for Excellence, 1889–1964*. Washington, DC: Georgetown University Press, 2010.

———. *A History of Georgetown University*. Vol. 3, *The Rise to Prominence, 1964–1989*. Washington, DC: Georgetown University Press, 2010.

O'Neill, Paul R., and Paul K. Williams. *Georgetown University*. Charleston, SC: Arcadia, 2003.

Rothman, Adam, and Elsa Barraza Mendoza, eds. *Facing Georgetown's History: A Reader on Slavery and Reconciliation*. Washington, DC: Georgetown University Press, 2021.

Scott, Pamela, and Antoinette J. Lee. *Buildings of the District of Columbia*. New York: Oxford University Press, 1993.

Area I: Historic Campus Core

OLD NORTH

Feinstein, Michael D. *The Restoration and Renovation of Old North*. Washington, DC: Georgetown Office of University Relations, 1983. BFCSC/GUA.

Forgey, Benjamin. "A New Look for GU's Old North." *Washington Post*, November 2, 1983.

Rogers, Hope. "Georgetown Today." *Georgetown University Magazine*, September–October 1983. BFCSC/GUA.

Toporoff, Andrew. "Listening to Architecture: What Georgetown University Says Today." *The Hoya,* February 8, 2012.
Turner, Paul Venable. *Campus: An American Planning Tradition*. Cambridge, MA: MIT Press, 1984.

GERVASE HALL

"The College Infirmary." *Georgetown College Journal* 5, no. 9 (June 1877): 101.
"Georgetown University Will Improve Infirmary and Faculty House." *Washington Post*, April 7, 1929.
"Infirmary Garden." *Georgetown College Journal* 1, no. 5 (April 1873): 44.
Nevils, Coleman, SJ. *Miniatures of Georgetown, 1634–1934*. Washington, DC: Georgetown University Press, 1935.
"Two Priests Hurt in Fire at GU." *Washington Post*, December 16, 1973.

ISAAC HAWKINS HALL

Georgetown University. *Report of the Working Group on Slavery, Memory, and Reconciliation to the President of Georgetown University*. Washington, DC: Georgetown University Press, 2016.
"Jesuits Homeless, Rooms Destroyed; Nuremberg Papers Saved from Flames." *The Hoya*, February 28, 1947.

RYAN HALL

Eagan, Owen. "Reviving History with New Academy." *The Hoya*, March 3, 2015.
"Gift to Georgetown, New South Building to Be Ida M. Ryan Hall." *Washington Post*, July 13, 1905.
Nevils, W. Coleman, SJ. Letter to Father Repetti, March 8, 1949. Old South folder, BFCSC/GUA.
"The New South Hall." *Georgetown College Journal* 33, no. 6 (March 1905): 234–36.

HEALY HALL

George, Hardy. "Georgetown University's Healy Building." *Journal of the Society of Architectural Historians* 31, no. 3 (October 1972): 208–16.
"The Georgetown University, A Realization of the Dream of Archbishop Carroll." *Washington Post*, March 18, 1878.
"New College Building at Georgetown, D.C., Messrs. Smithmeyer & Pelz, Architects." *American Architect and Building News* 7, no. 122 (March 27, 1880): 129.
"Notes on the New Building." *Georgetown College Journal* 7, no. 6 (April 1879): 1.
Prelinger, Elizabeth. "From Her Spires and Steeples Beaming: Mission and Image in Bricks and Stone." In *Georgetown at Two Hundred: Faculty Reflections on the University's Future,* edited by William McFadden, 335–53. Washington, DC: Georgetown University Press, 1990.
Riley, Brenda, and Jon Reynolds. "Riggs Library Reopens." *Georgetown Magazine*, November–December 1982. BFCSC/GUA.

US Commission of Fine Arts. *Georgetown Architecture, Northwest Washington, District of Columbia: Historic American Buildings Survey*. Washington, DC: National Park Service, 1970.

DAHLGREN CHAPEL

Collier, Robert J. "The Dahlgren Memorial Chapel." *Georgetown College Journal* 20, no. 8 (May 1892): 175–77.

LoLordo, Ann. "Tabernacle, Stained Glass Windows to Stay in Chapel." *The Hoya*, February 15, 1974. BFCSC/GUA.

Watkins, Anna. *A History of Dahlgren Chapel*. Washington, DC: Georgetown University, 2009. BFCSC/GUA.

Area II: Copley and Beyond

GATEHOUSES

"Archaic Entrance Replaced by Highway." *The Hoya*, September 29, 1955.

"Booth Has Gifts, Information." *The Hoya*, October 6, 1960.

"Death of a Good Man." *Georgetown College Journal*, August–October 1876, 2–3.

"The Georgetown College Cadets." *Georgetown College Journal*, May 1877, 1.

POULTON HALL

"Electronic Language Teaching System Starts at G.U." *Washington Post*, November 22, 1950.

COPLEY HALL

Bowen, John G. "Copley Hall." *Georgetown College Journal*, April 1933, 418–26.

"Rev. Wm. Cowardin Laid at Rest." *The Hoya*, February 20, 1925.

WHITE-GRAVENOR HALL

Bowen, John G. "The White Gravenor Building." *Georgetown College Journal*, March 1933, 319–24.

"New G.U. Building Soon to Be Ready." *Washington [DC] Star*, March 18, 1933.

DAVIS PERFORMING ARTS CENTER

Doherty, William B. "The Trophy Room." *Georgetown College Journal*, November 1908, 45–46. Ryan Gym folder, BFCSC/GUA.

Dunlap, David W. "Hugh Hardy, 84, City Landmarks' Theatrical Architect." *New York Times*, March 19, 2017.

"Farewell to Ryan." Cornerstone Ceremony Program for McDonough Gymnasium, October 1950. Ryan Post-Gym folder, BFCSC/GUA.

Forgey, Benjamin. "Little Cause for Applause: GU Theater Hits a Brick Wall, but Its Interior Merits a Bow." *Washington Post*, March 5, 2006.

"Ryan Administration Building." Ryan Post-Gym folder, BFCSC/GUA.
"Ryan Gym at Georgetown U. Remodeled for Basketball Games." *Washington Post*, January 14, 1940.
"Ryan Gymnasium to Serve in New Role." *Georgetown Record*, September 1952. Ryan Post-Gym folder, BFCSC/GUA.

EDWARD B. BUNN, SJ, INTERCULTURAL CENTER

Forgey, Benjamin. "The Inside Story." *Washington Post*, November 19, 1988.
Kitsok, Greg. "Intercultural Bids Top Budget." *The Hoya*, March 14, 1980.
Telerski, Noah. "The Sun Also Rises: Georgetown's Long and Complicated History of Solar Energy." *Georgetown Voice*, March 15, 2019.

Area III: Central Campus and West Campus

REISS SCIENCE BUILDING

"Role of Science at GU Cited by Dr. Seaborg in Dedication Address." *The Hoya*, October 18, 1962.
Rothman, Adam. "The Price of Georgetown: A Walking Tour of Slavery, Memory, and Reconciliation at Georgetown University." With contributions by students. Accessed 2023, https://slaveryarchive.georgetown.edu/items/show/505.

PEDRO ARRUPE, SJ, RESIDENCE HALL

Burgoa, Lisa. "Exclusive: Human Remains Found During Construction of Residence Hall, Which Sits Near Segregated Graveyard Where Georgetown Slaves Were Buried." *The Hoya*, August 8, 2018.
Burgoon, Lauren. "Remembering Jesuits Second Founder." Georgetown University, accessed 2023, https://president.georgetown.edu/1242664145353–2/.
Gandhi, Maya. "Arrupe Hall Fails ADA Compliance Standards." *The Hoya*, September 6, 2018.
Sasaki Design. "Georgetown University Pedro Arrupe, S.J., Hall." sasaki.com, accessed May 3, 2022, https://www.sasaki.com/projects/georgetown-university-pedro-arrupe-s-j-hall/.

HENLE VILLAGE

"Dorm Debuts on Time, Missing Finishing Touches." *The Hoya*, September 4, 1976.

DARNALL HALL

Canepa, Ellen. "Devron to Swing Schedule Gambol; Hoya Starchies." *The Hoya*, February 11, 1965.

REGENTS HALL

Patzer, Meghan. "Regents Hall Construction Will Finish Early." *The Hoya*, February 17, 2012.

LEAVEY STUDENT CENTER

Forgey, Benjamin. "The Inside Story: A Look at Georgetown's New Leavey Center." *Washington Post*, November 19, 1988.

RAFIK B. HARIRI BUILDING

Boniface, Russell. "Georgetown University's School of Business: Traditional, Modern, and Energy-Efficient." *AI Architect This Week*, September 25, 2009.

Dickerson, Justin. "Plans Advance for New MSB Home." *The Hoya*, April 20, 2004.

Goody Clancy. "Rafik B. Hariri Building, McDonough School of Business." Accessed May 3, 2022, https://www.goodyclancy.com/projects/rafik-b-hariri-building-mcdonough-school-of-business/.

Quotah, Eman. "Architects Design Headquarters for Business School." *Blue and Gray*, April 14, 2004.

Area IV: East Campus

Reiff, Daniel. *Washington Architecture, 1791–1861, Problems in Development*. Washington, DC: Commission of Fine Arts, 1971.

US Commission of Fine Arts. *Georgetown Architecture, Northwest Washington, District of Columbia: Historic American Buildings Survey Selections Number 10*. Washington, DC: National Park Service Office of Archeology and Historic Preservation, 1970.

ALUMNI SQUARE

Hurt, Harrison. "Facilities Negligence Endangers Students." *The Hoya*, February 22, 2019.

Jacobsen, Hugh Newell. *Hugh Newell Jacobsen, Architect*. Victoria, BC: Images, 2003.

O'Connor, Eileen O. "CAG Reacts to Village B Plan." *The Hoya*, September 28, 1979.

ROBERT AND BERNICE WAGNER ALUMNI HOUSE

Georgetown University Alumni Association. "GUAA History." Accessed May 15, 2022, https://alumni.georgetown.edu/alumni-association/history.

Outerbridge Horsey Associates PLLC. "Georgetown University Alumni House." Accessed May 15, 2022, http://www.outerbridgehorsey.com/projects/detail_guah.html.

NEVILS RESIDENCE HALL

Frederick, M. E. "Encountering the Haunting Spirit of Nevils Past." *Georgetown Voice*, March 2, 1976.

Fritschel, Heidi. "New Housing Goes Up on East Campus." *Georgetown University Magazine*, July–August 1983.

"G.U. Spending $8 Million in New Developments." November 8, 1957. Nevils Building folder, BFCSC/GUA.

Held, Ivan. "Nevils as Dorm Soon." *The Hoya*, December 1, 1978.

"School of Medicine—The Proposed Hospital." *Georgetown College Journal*, March 1897, 76–77.

EDMUND A. WALSH MEMORIAL BUILDING

"Georgetown University Dedicates Building to Reverend Edmund Walsh." *Deltasig of Delta Sigma Pi*, May 1959, 103–4.

"It's a Big World at GU, but It Spins the Wrong Way." *Washington Post*, September 27, 1958.

Jonnalagadda, Deepika. "Walsh Art Gallery to Open Next Semester After Delay." *The Hoya*, November 17, 2017.

Kumpka, Peter J. "Ike Speaks at Dedication." *Baltimore Sun*, October 14, 1958.

CAR BARN

EHT Traceries Historic Preservation. "Georgetown Car Barn." Accessed 2018–19, https://www.traceries.com/projects/georgetown-car-barn/.

Wallender, Andrew. "University Completes Two-Year Renovation of Car Barn First Floor." *The Hoya*, January 31, 2017.

Area V: South Campus

LAUINGER LIBRARY

Bademli, Irmak. "Lovely or Lackluster: The History Behind Lauinger Library's Architectural Design." *The Hoya*, January 28, 2003.

Conway, Lynn. *In the Aggregate: The Planning and Building of Lauinger Library* (Lauinger Library's Thirty-Fifth Anniversary). Online exhibition, October 1–December 31, 2005. https://library.georgetown.edu/exhibition/aggregate-planning-and-building-lauinger-library-lauinger-librarys-thirty-fifth.

———. *50 Years of Excellence and Service*. Gallery and online exhibitions, February 3–July 30, 2020. Charles Marvin Fairchild Memorial Gallery Special Collections.

Curran, Pat. "Lauinger: The Past, Present and Future of Georgetown's 'Ugly' Library." *The Hoya*, August 29, 2014.

Davis, Jon. "Enthusiastic Response Greets Library Opening." *The Hoya*, April 16, 1970.

"Dedication of New Library Held in Gaston." *The Hoya*, April 30, 1970.

Gyure, Dale Allen. "The Heart of the University: A History of the Library as an Architectural Symbol of American Higher Education." *Winterthur Portfolio* 42 (Summer–Autumn 2008): 107–32.

"Library Architect Named." *Georgetown Record* (July 1965): 1. Lauinger Library folder, BFCSC/GUA.

McCullough, Gerard. "District Fine Arts Commission Approves Library." *The Hoya*, September 29, 1966.

Von Eckardt, Wolf. "College Library Caught in City's Planning Vise." *Washington Post*, June 7, 1966.

———. "Part of the Setting, like the Ivy." *Washington Post*, April 17, 1970.

VILLAGE A

Gordon, Peter. "Village A Builders Uncooperative." *Georgetown Voice*, September 16, 1980.

Grimes, William. "John Carl Warnecke, Architect to Kennedy, Dies at 91." *New York Times*, April 23, 2010.

Nucci, Robert. "Village A Finally Opens." *Georgetown Voice*, October 2, 1979.

Whitehead, Liz. "Village A: New Dates Set." *Georgetown Voice*, September 11, 1979.

———. "Village A to Open 1–4 Months Late." *Georgetown Voice*, August 24, 1979.

NEW SOUTH

Fitzgerald, James V. "Cafeteria Will Serve 6,500 Meals Daily in New South Building." *Georgetown Record*, December 1959. BFCSC/GUA.

HEALEY FAMILY STUDENT CENTER

Goldchain, Michelle. "Georgetown University Wins 3 AIA Awards for Student Center." November 25, 2015, dc.curbed.com.

Georgetown University. "History of the HFSC." Georgetown University, accessed 2022, https://studentcenters.georgetown.edu/ourspaces/hfsc/history/.

Richardson, Katherine. "HFSC Opens to Students." *The Hoya*, September 9, 2014.

WOLFINGTON HALL

Eagan, Owen. "Reviving History with New Academy." *The Hoya*, March 3, 2015.

Kleinrock Studio Architecture PLCC. "Georgetown University Jesuit Community Residence." Accessed 2022, http://www.kleinrockstudio.com/project1-13.html.

Lewis, Rebekah. "Your Inside Look at the Southwest Quad." *The Hoya*, August 22, 2003.

Robert A. M. Stern Architects LLP. "Southwest Quadrangle Georgetown University." ramsa.com, https://www.ramsa.com/projects/project/southwest-quadrangle.

Area VI: Southwest Campus

ANNE MARIE BECRAFT HALL

Jaster, Emily. "University Renames Freedom and Remembrance Halls in Honor of Descendants of 1838 Slave Sale." *Georgetown Voice*, April 25, 2017.

Verveer, Melanne. "Viewpoint: Celebrating Anne Marie Becraft." *The Hoya*, April 18, 2017.

HARBIN HALL

Bunn, E. B., SJ, Letter to Rev. T. Byron Collins, February 8, 1963. Harbin Hall folder, BFCSC/GUA.

"Harbin Hall Opening Ceremony." 1965. Harbin Hall folder, BFCSC/GUA.

"Harbin Residence Hall Formally Opened; New Design Comfortably Accommodates 426." *Georgetown Record*, December 1965.

"New Men's Dorm." *Georgetown Courier*, December 1964.

Rector Letter to Jim FitzGerald, November 27, 1963. Harbin Hall folder, BFCSC /GUA.

Robinson, K. G. Letter to Madden, architect, October 16, 1964. Harbin Hall folder, BFCSC/GUA.

Yanni, Carla. *Living on Campus: An Architectural History of the American Dormitory.* Minneapolis: University of Minnesota Press, 2019.

VILLAGE C

Georgetown University. "Village C West Residential Living." Accessed July 17, 2020. https://residentialliving.georgetown.edu/communities/firstyear/vcw/.

Georgetown University Libraries. "Where on Campus Was the O'Gara Building and for Whom Was It Named?" (n.d.). https://www.library.georgetown.edu/infrequently-asked-questions/where-campus-was-ogara-building-and-whom-was-it-named.

Lee, Kenneth. "The Four Freshmen Dorms." *Georgetown Voice*, August 1, 2015.

SOUTHWEST QUADRANGLE

Lewis, Rebekah. "Your Inside Look at the Southwest Quad." *The Hoya*, August 22, 2003.

Robert A. M. Stern Architects, LLP. "Southwest Quadrangle Georgetown University." Accessed 2022, https://www.ramsa.com/projects/project/southwest-quadrangle.

Timiraos, Nick. "From Hole to Home, Southwest Quad Completed." *The Hoya*, August 22, 2003.

Area VII: West Campus: Sports and Observatory

MCDONOUGH GYMNASIUM

DC Office of Planning. "Leon Chatelain Jr." *DC Architects Directory*. Washington, DC: Historic Preservation Office, 2010.

"G.U. Alumni to Open $800,000 Fund Drive for Memorial Gym." *The Hoya*, November 1947.

Hughes, Mike. "Gym Affords All Sports; Named After Fr. McDonough." *The Hoya*, September 17, 1951.

"Noted District Architect Leon Chatelain Jr. Dies." *Washington Post*, May 8, 1979.

Stack, Gene. "Gym to Be Finished by Summer." *The Hoya*, February 7, 1951.

White, Suzanne. "Inheriting History, After a Youthful Rebellion Against

Tradition, Architect Leon Chatelain III Saw the Bigger Picture." *Washington Business Journal*, May 24, 2004.

JOHN R. THOMPSON JR. INTERCOLLEGIATE ATHLETIC CENTER

Maguire, Carolyn. "IAC Named for Thompson, Jr." *The Hoya*, March 7, 2014.

Privitera, Sherri. "How the Thompson Center Takes Georgetown Athletics to New Heights." populous.com, accessed October 6, 2016. https://populous.com/thompson-center-takes-georgetown-athletics-new-heights.

Wang, Gene. "Georgetown University to Break Ground on Athletics Facility." *Washington Post*, March 3, 2014.

HEYDEN OBSERVATORY

Georgetown College Astronomical Observatory. *Annals of the Astronomical Observatory of Georgetown College*. New York: Edward Dunigan & Brother, 1852. BFCSC/GUA.

Heyden, Francis J., SJ. *The Beginning and End of a Jesuit Observatory*. n.d. Observatory Building folder, BFCSC/GUA.

YATES FIELD HOUSE

Glod, Maria. "Architect Creates a New Spiritual Foundation." *Washington Post*, February 18, 2004.

Hall, Loretta. *Underground Buildings: More Than Meets the Eye*. Fresno, CA: Quill Driver, 2004.

Randolph, Katherine. "Kehoe Field Renovation Project Set to Begin in 2019." *Georgetown Voice*, December 6, 2018.

Thomas, Connor. "Kehoe to Close for Renovations in February, Details Near Finalization." *The Hoya*, December 7, 2018.

Areas VIII and IX: Medical Center, Law Center, and Capitol Campus

"Architect Vlastimil Koubek Dies at 75." *Washington Post*, February 18, 2003.

Biemiller, Lawrence. "Georgetown U's Law School Gets a Campus at Last." *Chronicle of Higher Education*, August 12, 2005.

Forgey, Benjamin. "Georgetown Law's Happy Campus." *Washington Post*, November 8, 1997.

McFadden, W. C., ed. *Georgetown at Two Hundred: Faculty Reflections on the University's Future*. Washington, DC: Georgetown University Press, 1990.

McIntosh, Kerry. "Law Buildings Completed." *The Hoya*, August 27, 2004.

Navera, Tristan. "Georgetown University Files Plans to Convert 111 Massachusetts, the Darth Vader Building, into Academic Space." *Washington Business Journal*, October 4, 2023.

Index

About the Author

Stephanie Rufino is an architectural historian and has published on the decoration and architecture of both the Washington National Cathedral and historic American banks from the 1920s. Dr. Rufino holds a PhD in American art and architectural history from the University of Virginia and an MBA from Georgetown University's McDonough School of Business. She graduated cum laude from Smith College and also earned a master's degree in art history. Dr. Rufino taught architectural history at Georgetown for a decade, where she also served in multiple university administrative roles. She currently serves as director of Undergraduate Design Programs and associate professor at the School of Architecture & Design at Wentworth in Boston.